The Visual Dictionary of Interior Architecture and Design

An AVA Book
Published by AVA Publishing SA
Rue des Fontenailles 16
Case Postale
1000 Lausanne 6
Switzerland
Tel: +41 786 005 109
Email: enquiries@avabooks.ch

Distributed by Thames & Hudson (ex-North America)
181a High Holborn
London WC1V 7QX
United Kingdom
Tel: +44 20 7845 5000
Fax: +44 20 7845 5055
Email: sales@thameshudson.co.uk
www.thamesandhudson.com

Distributed in the USA & Canada by:
Ingram Publisher Services Inc.
1 Ingram Blvd.
La Vergne, TN 37086
USA
Tel: +001 866 400 5351
Fax: +001 800 838 1149
E-mail: customer.service@ingrampublisherservices.com

English Language Support Office
AVA Publishing (UK) Ltd.
Tel: +44 1903 204 455
Email: enquiries@avabooks.ch

Copyright © AVA Publishing SA 2009

All rights reserved. No part of this publication may be
reproduced, stored in a retrieval system or transmitted in
any form or by any means, electronic, mechanical,
photocopying, recording or otherwise, without permission of
the copyright holder.

ISBN 978-2-940373-80-2 and 2-940373-80-9

10 9 8 7 6 5 4 3 2 1

Design by Gavin Ambrose
www.gavinambrose.co.uk

Production by AVA Book Production Pte. Ltd., Singapore
Tel: +65 6334 8173
Fax: +65 6259 9830
Email: production@avabooks.com.sg

All reasonable attempts have been made to trace, clear and
credit the copyright holders of the images reproduced in this
book. However, if any credits have been inadvertently
omitted, the publisher will endeavour to incorporate
amendments in future editions.

The Visual Dictionary of Interior Architecture and Design

How to get the most out of this book 4

This book is an easy-to-use reference to the key terms used in interior architecture and design. Each entry comprises a brief textual definition along with an illustration or visual example of the point under discussion. Supplementary contextual information is also included.

Key areas addressed in this book are those terms commonly used in reference to interior architecture and design, history and production.

Entries are presented in alphabetical order to provide an easy reference system.

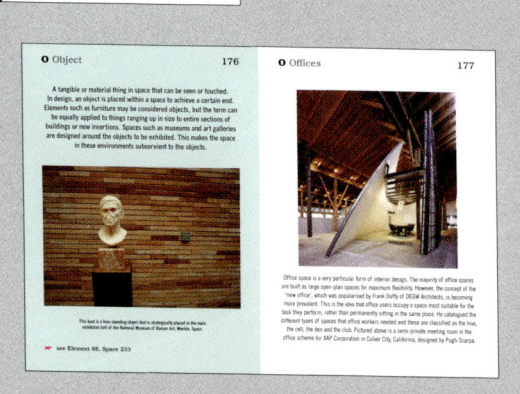

5

R Rotunda 218

A circular building, or part of a building, may be described as a rotunda. This structure is usually, though not always, covered with a dome. The rotunda is a feature of many different styles of architecture, but it is most prevalent within the classical style.

The interior of the rotunda of the Texan Capitol Building, Dallas, USA

☞ see Classical 52, Dome 76

R Rural Studio 219

An American 'design and build' practice with a conscience, founded in 1993 by the late Sam Mockbee, whose own upbringing in segregated Mississippi gave him great awareness of the injustices of life in southern USA. Rural Studio builds unique homes and community buildings such as that illustrated for poor communities in western Alabama. These homes are constructed from reused and recycled materials to create cheap, yet well-designed and well-constructed houses.

Each page or double-page spread contains a single entry and, where appropriate, a printer's hand symbol ☞ provides page references to other related and relevant entries.

A timeline of key interior architecture and design movements, personalities and influences helps to provide historical context for selected moments in the discipline's development.

Introduction

Welcome to *The Visual Dictionary of Interior Architecture and Design*, a book that provides textual definitions and visual explanations for common terms found in the key areas of interior architecture, interior design and interior decoration, as well as entries from the art and design world in general.

This book aims to provide a clear understanding of the many terms that are commonly misused or confused, pointing out the distinction between modernism and postmodernism, art deco and art nouveau, as well as the differences in approaches to, for example, artificial and natural light when used in interiors. *The Visual Dictionary of Interior Architecture and Design* illustrates these definitions with photographs and drawings, as well as key examples of forms of design.

Left: Rachel Whiteread's installation in the Turbine Hall of the Tate Modern, London, by Herzog & de Meuron, emphasises the flexibility of the cavernous interior of the Turbine Hall.

Facing page: Foster Associates have deliberately contrasted the new and shiny elements of the remodelled interior with the decaying body of the old Boiler House at the Essen Design Centre in Germany.

7

8

An understanding of these terminologies will help you to comprehend the world in which interior designers work and also enable you to articulate, communicate and realise your ideas.

The design of interiors is a discipline that has been practised much but theorised little. It has developed recently as an independent and fully recognised area of design in its own right. There are many parallels between interior architecture, interior design and interior decoration, which should be defined here first.

Facing page: The rigid and orthogonal organisation of the interior space of the Barcelona Pavilion is softened by the deployment of a sumptuous red curtain.

Top left: The interior of the Castelvecchio Museum, Verona, Italy, by Carlo Scarpa. The new flooring skirts around the existing building, separating the existing and the new.

Top right: The ornate entrance hall of the House of Scientists Lviv, Ukraine, built in 1898.

Each area deals with the transformation of a given space, whether that is the crumbling ruins of an ancient building or the drawn parameters of a new building. This alteration or conversion is a complex process of understanding the qualities of the existing building, while simultaneously accommodating this understanding within the functional requirements of the new.

Interior decoration is the art of decorating interior spaces or rooms to create a specific atmosphere to fit well with the existing architecture. It is concerned with issues such as surface pattern, ornament, furniture, soft furnishings, lighting and materials.

Interior design is an interdisciplinary practice that addresses the creation of interior environments through the manipulation of spatial volume, placement of specific elements, furniture and treatment of surfaces. It generally describes projects that require little or no structural changes to the existing building.

Interior architecture is concerned with the remodelling of existing buildings and the attitude towards existing spaces and structures. It bridges the practices of interior design and architecture, often dealing with complex structural, environmental and servicing problems.

Facing page: The staircase in the interior of the Casa De Musica in Porto is constructed from concrete and clad in steel with a glass balustrade. It was designed by Rem Koolhaas/OMA.

11

Contents

Prologue
How to get the most out of this book ... 4
Introduction ... 6

The Dictionary ... 16

A
Acoustics ... 18
Alessi ... 19
Anthropometrics ... 20
Applied Texture ... 21
Arch ... 22
Archigram ... 23
Architectural Promenade ... 24
Architecture ... 25
Architrave ... 26
Art Deco ... 27
Art Nouveau ... 28
Arts and Crafts ... 29
Atkinson, Robert ... 30
Atrium ... 31
Avant-Garde ... 32

B
Balustrade ... 33
Banister ... 34
Baroque ... 35
Bauhaus ... 36
Bay ... 37
Beam ... 38
BIDA and ASID ... 39
Branding ... 40
Brutalism ... 41
Building ... 42
Building and Planning Regulations ... 43
Byzantine ... 44

C
Canali, Guido ... 45
Cantilever ... 46
Casson Mann ... 47
Ceiling ... 48
Chair ... 49
Circulation ... 50
Cladding ... 51
Classical ... 52
Climate ... 53
Coates, Nigel ... 54
Colombo, Joe ... 55
Colour ... 56
Column ... 57
Conran, Terence ... 58
Conservation ... 59
Constructivism ... 60
Context ... 61
Cooling ... 62
Cornice ... 63
Corridor ... 64
Counterpoint ... 65
Coving ... 66
Crawford, Ilse ... 67
Curious Boym ... 68
Curtains ... 69

D
Deconstruction ... 70
Design ... 71
De Stijl ... 72
Detail ... 73
Diller Scofidio + Renfro ... 74
Disability Legislation ... 75
Dome ... 76
Domestic ... 77
Donald, Stephen ... 78
Door ... 79
Drainage ... 80

Drawing	81	Gesamtkunstwerk	116
Droog Design	82	Golden Section	117
Duchamp, Marcel	83	Gothic Revival	118
Dwelling	84	Graphic Design	119
E		Gray, Eileen	120
Eames, Charles and Ray	85	Guixé, Martí	121
Edge	86	**H**	
Edwardian	87	Heating	122
Element	88	Hejduk, John	123
Elevation	89	Hierarchy	124
Enfilade	90	History	125
Engineering: Civil	91	Holl, Steven	126
Engineering: Electrical	92	Hyper-Reality	127
Engineering: Mechanical	93	**I**	
Engineering: Structural	94	Insertion	128
Environmental Control	95	Installation	129
Ergonomics	96	Interior Architecture	130
Ethics	97	Interior Decoration	131
Exhibition Design	98	Interior Design	132
F		Interior Education	133
Façade	99	International Style	134
FAT	100	Intervention	135
Floor	101	**J**	
Floor Covering	102	Jekyll, Gertrude	136
Form	103	Jiřičná, Eva	137
Formalism	104	Judd, Donald	138
Form Follows Form	105	**K**	
Form Follows Function	106	Kelly, Ben	139
Found Texture	107	Klein Dytham Architecture	140
Framing	108	Klein, Yves	141
Free Plan	109	Koolhaas, Rem	142
Fresco	110	Kroll, Lucien	143
Frieze	111	**L**	
Function	112	Land Design Studio	144
Furniture	113	Le Corbusier	145
G		Light: Artificial	146
Gensler	114	Light: Natural	147
Geometry	115	Listed/Protected Buildings	148

Llewelyn-Bowen, Lawrence	149	Openings	178
Load Bearing	150	Ornament	179
Loos, Adolf	151	**P**	
LOT-EK	152	Painting	180
Louvres	153	Palladio, Andrea	181
Lumsden at	154	Partition	182
Small Back Room		Pattern	183
M		Perriand, Charlotte	184
Machine Aesthetic	155	Perspective	185
Mackintosh,	156	Piano Nobile	186
Charles Rennie		Piloti	187
Magazines	157	Plan	188
Mannerism	158	Plane	189
Mare, André	159	Ponti, Giò	190
Materials:	160–161	Portico	191
Brick		Post and Beam	192
Concrete		Postmodernism	193
Glass		Prefabricated	194
Plastic		Presentation	195
Stone		Private/Public	196
Timber		Product Design	197
Matta Clark, Gordon	162	Proportion	198
Mezzanine	163	Psychology	199
Mies van der Rohe, Ludwig	164	**Q**	
Minimalism	165	Quadrangle	200
Mirror	166	Qualification	201
Model	167	Quatrefoil	202
Modernism	168–169	Quoin	203
Modular	170	**R**	
Morris, William	171	Ranalli, George	204
Movement	172	Randy Brown Associates	205
N		Raumplan	206
Narrative	173	Reflection	207
Nash, John	174	Regency	208
Novembre, Fabio	175	Reichen et Robert	209
O		Remodelling	210
Object	176	Renaissance	211
Offices	177	Restoration	212

Retail Design	213	**U**	
Reuse	214	Universal Design Studio	249
Rococo	215	Urbanism	250
Roman	216	Utopia	251
Room	217	**V**	
Rotunda	218	Ventilation	252
Rural Studio	219	Vernacular	253
Ruskin, John	220	Victorian	254
S		View	255
Sample	221	Villa	256
Scale	222	Vitra	257
Scarpa, Carlo	223	Volume	258
Scheme	224	**W**	
Section	225	Wall	259
Semper, Gottfried	226	Wall Covering	260
Sequence	227	Wharton, Edith	261
Served/Servant Space	228	Whiteread, Rachel	262
Skirting	229	Window	263
Soffit	230	Wolfe, Elsie de	264
Softroom	231	Wrapping	265
Sottsass, Ettore	232	Wright, Frank Lloyd	266
Space	233	**X**	
Stack Effect	234	Xenakis, Iannis	267
Stairs	235	**Y**	
Starck, Philippe	236	Yasui, Hideo	268
Structure	237	Yoshioka, Tokujin	269
Surface	238	**Z**	
Sustainability	239	Zeitgeist	270
Symmetry	240	Zoomorphic	271
T			
Tactics	241	**The Details**	
Tension	242	The Timeline	274
Textile Design	243	Credits	284
Texture	244	Conclusion	286
Theatre Design	245	Acknowledgements	287
Threshold	246	Index of Synonyms and Cross References	288
Truss	247		
Tudor	248		

The Dictionary

A Acoustics 18

The seats in the hall of the Welsh Millennium Centre are designed to absorb sound and avoid echoes.

The processes, materials and interior features used to control the nature and propagation of sound. For example, acoustic panels buffer, direct or reflect sound in a concert hall in order to create the correct level of amplification from the position of the audience. The aim of acoustics in this instance is to improve and amplify sound, whereas in a recording studio, for example, the desired effect is to muffle and absorb sound to avoid echoes and feedback and ensure a clean recording.

A Alessi 19

Founded in 1921, the Italian design company Alessi set out to produce expertly crafted cutlery and metal tableware; its range has expanded greatly and now includes designs for house and kitchen products too. Alessi creations are produced in stainless steel and complementary metals, plastic, wood, crystal and porcelain. It uses high profile product designers and architects to produce ranges for its brand. Some of the world's most distinguished designers, including Philippe Starck, Ettore Sottsass and Michael Graves, have all produced objects for Alessi. Pictured below is the coffee.it espresso coffee maker, designed for Alessi by Wiel Arets.

☛ see Sottsass, Ettore 232, Starck, Philippe 236

A Anthropometrics 20

The comparative study of the sizes and proportions of the human form. In design, anthropometrics is used to determine the size of objects and spaces in relation to the human body. The phrase 'human scale' refers to objects of a certain anthropometric proportion that is immediately related to the body so that objects and spaces can be effectively and comfortably used by humans.

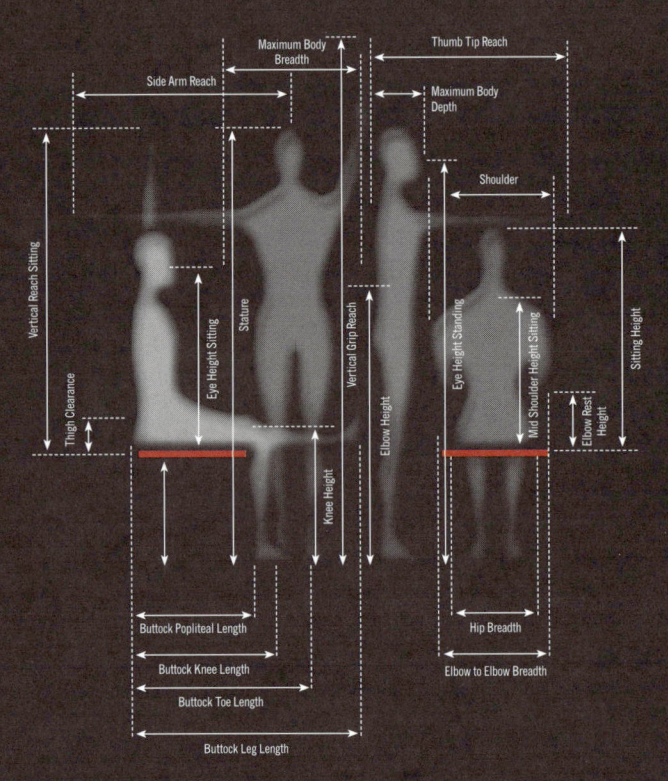

see Proportion 198, Scale 222

A Applied Texture 21

Similar to applied decoration, applied texture is the act of applying a textural material to a surface, with the intention of aesthetically enhancing the surface. Applied texture may be used to define a certain area in order to make it distinct from its surroundings; it may be to draw attention to it or to distract attention from other aspects of the surroundings. Contrasting textures can create interest in a surface that may not otherwise exist.

The rear wall of the Santa Caterina Market, Barcelona, by EMBT, has an abstract pattern of pieces of masonry and stone applied in order to enliven the nondescript plane.

see Surface 238

A Arch 22

The arch is an element that is used to make an opening in a load-bearing structure. It consists of a curved or pointed arrangement that diverts the load around the opening. Arches commonly feature in church architecture and industrial structures, particularly railway bridges and viaducts.

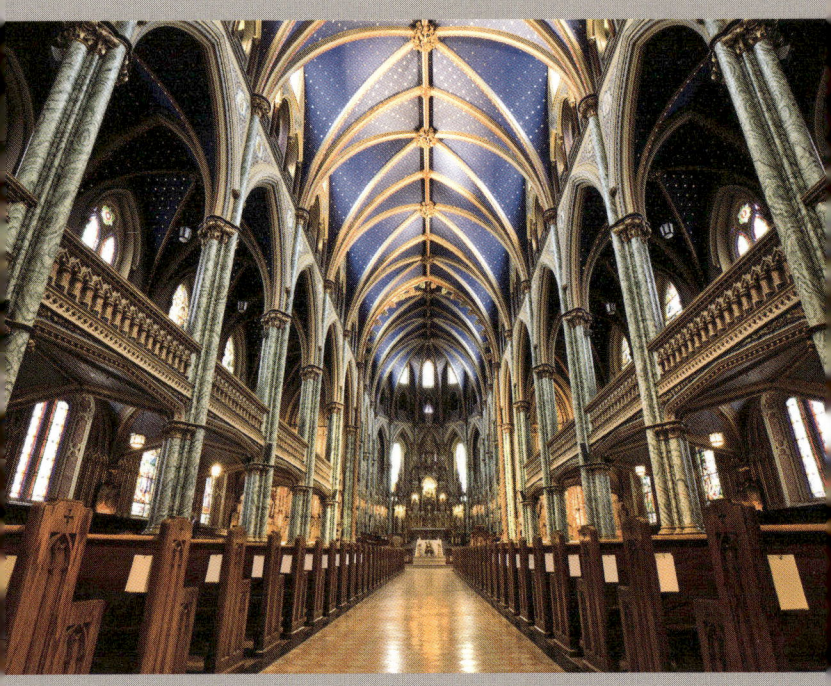

The arches of Notre Dame Basilica in Ottawa, Canada, have weight-bearing qualities but also create a decorative effect.

see Load Bearing 150, Structure 237

A Archigram

Future City, a theoretical student project inspired by Archigram's *Walking City*.

A 1960s British architecture collective and the name of an alternative architecture journal published by the group. Archigram was a reaction to the accepted precepts of architecture, in both modern and post-war Britain.

Peter Cook, one of the most prolific writers of the group, described the Bauhaus as 'an insult to functionalism' and advocated the opportunities that modern materials and production provided. The group's manifesto was used to suggest an alternative mode of thinking about architecture. While Archigram did not leave any physical mark on architecture, it influenced future 'star architects' such as Norman Foster, Zaha Hadid and Will Alsop.

☛ see Bauhaus 36, Modernism 168–169

A Architectural Promenade 24

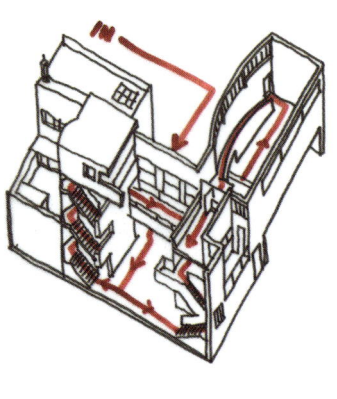

A device used to arrange space within a building to gain the most dramatic effect. The architectural promenade is an arrangement of rooms, spaces, views and sightlines that open up for the user as they move (or promenade) through a space. A true architectural promenade creates unexpected views and perspectives that force the viewer to constantly notice and reassess the building.

In the Villa La Roche (pictured above), Le Corbusier created an architectural promenade that would display the works of art housed within it. The promenade leads the visitor up and down staircases, over ramps, into tight spaces, across balconies and through open spaces.

☛ see Space 233, View 255

A Architecture

The Kijk-Kubus in Rotterdam, Holland (pictured above), shows the fundamentally formal qualities of architecture and how the shape of the exterior can influence the design of the interior.

The word architecture originates from the Greek word *arkhitekton*, meaning master builder. Often described as the mother of the arts, it tells the story of human history. Architecture in relation to interior design and building reuse is the context in which the interior designer works. It is the immediate environment to which the interior designer responds; it will influence the nature of the interior and inform the interrelationship between a new use and an existing context.

see Context 61, Interior Design 132

A Architrave 26

A term used to refer to the structure and surround of a doorway. It describes the frame, beading, jamb and abutment of the doorway, all of which are used primarily to disguise the join between the surface of the wall plaster and the doorframe.

In the context of classical Greco-Roman architecture, an architrave is a lintel that sits above a row of columns, supporting the pediment, frieze and cornice of a building while stringing the columns together.

The surrounding architrave of the doorway of the eleventh-century Aljaferia Palace in Zaragoza, Spain, is elaborately ornate and grandly announces the opening between two rooms.

☞ see Column 57, Cornice 63, Frieze 111

A Art Deco 27

A style of design that proliferated throughout Europe and North America in the early 1900s. A branch of modernism, art deco was an aesthetic that combined many features of contemporaneous movements, such as art nouveau, cubism and Futurism. The name is derived from the Paris-based 1925 Exposition Internationale des Arts Décoratifs et Industriels Modernes. Crisp lines and geometric shapes such as those seen at the De La Warr Pavilion at Bexhill-on-Sea in the UK (shown here), are typical of the art deco style.

see Art Nouveau 28

A Art Nouveau

Dating from 1890 to 1914, the organic, highly stylised, flowing forms of art nouveau were a reaction to the mass industrialisation and consumerisation of craft that had taken place in the nineteenth century. In fine art, art nouveau was embraced by Impressionists such as Edouard Manet. The work of Hector Guimard, the creator of the famous signage for the Paris Métro stations, produced one of the most recognisable forms of the art nouveau aesthetic. In the Victor Horta House in Brussels (shown here), organic fronds of decorative steel and timber, typical of the art nouveau style, are used to great effect.

A Arts and Crafts

The entrance hall and stairs to the upper floor of Red House in Kent in the UK, evoke rustic and vernacular languages in order to promote simplicity and craftsmanship in design.

A largely British and American movement that sought to develop a new form of moral design. Key proponents of the movement, such as William Morris and John Ruskin, abhorred the consequences of the Industrial Revolution, both architecturally and socially. Their response to this was to reinstate the skill of craftsmanship within architecture. This idea was taken almost literally in the case of Philip Webb and William Morris's Red House (1859).

☛ see Morris, William 171, Ruskin, John 220

A Atkinson, Robert

A prolific British designer of the inter-war period, Robert Atkinson (1883–1952) is best known for his art deco interior of the Daily Express building on Fleet Street, London. The building itself, designed by Sir Owen Williams in 1932, is a glorious steel and glass construction with curving forms, typical of the art deco style. Atkinson's 1930s Hollywood-inspired interior (shown here) includes a reception raised on a black marble plinth, a backlit ceiling in silver and gold, and walls of rosewood and chrome detailing.

see Art Deco 27

A Atrium 31

Atriums were first used in Roman times as inner courtyards in domestic buildings. They were open to the sky and surrounded by an overhanging roof. The term is now used to describe a large internal public space, often the full height of the building and with a glazed roof. The atrium allows natural light to penetrate deep into the heart of the building; it will often contain elements of circulation, such as stairs and elevators and sometimes even a garden. It is usually the central focus of a large building and will have rooms opening on to it on many levels.

A large atrium allows light to cascade down through the interior of a building and animate the journey through it.

A Avant-Garde 32

The Viennese designers Coop Himmelb(l)au are regarded as progressive and radical. The new museum pavilion in Groningen, the Netherlands, which was designed to hold old master paintings, is particularly typical of their dynamic and avant-garde approach.

A French term describing those ahead of their time, the avant-garde encompasses all those advocating progress and hints at a degree of eccentricity and *joie de vivre*. The avant-garde shifts with each development or acceptance of a genre. The modernists, for example, were considered avant-garde in the early part of the twentieth century; however, by the 1970s, modernism had become the architecture of choice.

☞ see Modernism 168–169

B Balustrade 33

A balustrade is the ornamental rail running up and around an exterior balcony or staircase, landing and stairwell. While having a practical use (to stop people falling down or off a staircase), it can also fulfil an ornamental or formal function – perhaps indicating the direction of the head and foot of a stair.

The solid, colourful, steel balustrade of the Staatsgalerie in Stuttgart is designed to not only stop people falling, but to also aid the flow of visitors around the edge of the rotunda.

☞ see Stairs 235

B Banister

The highly decorated banister in the Zacherl-Haus, Vienna, by Jože Plečnik, is typical of his vernacular-inspired work.

A modification of the word 'baluster' (the baluster is a single upright joint in a banister or balustrade), a banister fulfils the same function as a balustrade. The term is used to refer to the balustrade element when used in an interior environment. In domestic architecture, a banister is traditionally an ornamental feature made of wood with a carved handrail, although many contemporary commercial interiors use glass or steel. There are many regulations governing the height and spacing of balustrades.

see Balustrade 33

B Baroque

A period in architectural history that began in the seventeenth century in Italy and spread quickly throughout Europe. The word baroque is derived from the Italian *barocco*, a medieval term meaning an obstacle to logic. The style emerged in the process of intertwining painting, sculpture and architecture. The majority of Rome's urban design (St Peter's Basilica in the Vatican, for example) is baroque in origin. The works of Bernini (1598–1680), especially the Sant'Andrea al Quirinale, are exemplars of the style.

The dramatic and exuberant interior of the Karlskirche, Vienna, by Fischer Von Erlach, unites architecture, interior space, sculpture and painting into one glorious whole.

B Bauhaus

a designers' collective and hugely influential school of architecture and design, the bauhaus operated in germany between 1919 and 1933. it was first established in weimar, and was born out of the arbeitsrat für kunst (workers' council for art). the bauhaus rejected decorative detailing and instead favoured simple geometric forms such as smooth façades and cubic shapes. members of the school included marcel breuer, mies van der rohe, lászló moholy-nagy, wassily kandinsky and adolf meyer. the bauhaus is often represented by the three coloured shapes shown below. these were developed by kandinsky, a prominent member of the school, as part of his colour-shape theory.

☞ see Mies van der Rohe, Ludwig 164

B Bay

When used in interiors, a bay can refer to two different elements. In a domestic environment it will refer to a bay window, commonly found in Victorian and Edwardian terraced houses. A bay window will usually be a two- or three-storey, three-sided protrusion from the face of the façade with a window in each side. A bay will also refer to a subdivision of a larger space but not enclosed on all sides. The smaller spaces between the structural columns within a framed building are referred to as individual bays.

The main living room of Hill House by Charles Rennie Mackintosh is dominated by the bay window that projects out of the building, forming an intimate space within the room.

see Edwardian 87, Façade 99, Victorian 254

B Beam 38

A horizontal structural element used in concert with
supporting walls or as part of a post-and-beam system.
A beam is also referred to as a lintel when it is positioned
above an opening in a wall. It is used to spread the load of
the wall above the sides of the opening. There are various
materials from which a beam can be made, most commonly
steel, concrete or wood.

☞ see Column 57, Load Bearing 150, Soffit 230, Structure 237

B BIDA and ASID

The British Interior Design Association was formed in 2002 and was set up for the purpose of encouraging and supporting excellence in interior design in the UK. While not regulated, the BIDA enforces a code of conduct, and full membership is limited to those with an interior design qualification and six years' experience.

The American Society of Interior Designers (ASID) was set up in 1975 and aims to engage its 40,000 members in a variety of professional programmes and activities through a network within the United States and Canada. The ASID is the oldest, largest professional organisation for interior designers in North America.

B Branding 40

The Apple Store on Fifth Avenue in New York is signalled to the street by a large simplified Apple sign, which hangs in the glass and steel entrance box. The logo is the brand identity of the company.

Branding is the process of creating a particular identity for a specific product, whether that is an object, a manufacturer or even a city. Within interior design and particularly the retail environment, the act of branding is something that advertisers do with a company or product. It is a process of establishing an idea, concept or a way of life behind the brand or logo. The concept of branding is currently very fashionable for cities; a city that is in the process of regeneration will try to rebrand itself to make its name synonymous with culture, shopping or city living.

B Brutalism

41

Derived from the French phrase béton brut, meaning 'raw concrete', brutalism was an architectural style that first appeared in the 1950s. Brutalist architecture uses hard, angular geometric forms and has a raw unfinished concrete aesthetic. The concrete may be inscribed with the impressions of the building process, such as the shuttering, or it may be deliberately left pitted and marked. It was a popular form of architecture used by municipal authorities in Britain for everything from bus stations to housing, but it became wildly unpopular with the British public in the 1970s for its hard and uncompromising aesthetic.

The raw and resolute concrete structure of the National Theatre by Denys Lasdun is a distinct landmark on the South Bank on the river Thames in London, UK.

B Building

A structure that is essentially constructed with walls and a roof, commonly created for human habitation or use. A building is the context within which interior designers work. The time taken to design and construct a building can vary greatly, depending on its size, complexity and cost. The fit-out of the interior is usually the final stage in the building process.

B Building and Planning Regulations

In many countries, architects and designers are required to work within a set of legal controls and guidelines.

Building regulations control the building and safety parameters of the construction process; building materials and elements must conform to various standards in order to be legally used in construction.

Planning regulations are set out by local and national governments to control the nature, aesthetic and impact of new and redeveloped buildings. Planning regulations might be used to protect historic areas from having their character damaged by new buildings or to prevent heavy industry being sited near residential areas.

B Byzantine

Pictured are the elegant and elaborate Byzantine domes and mosaics of the Blue Mosque of Istanbul.

A period in history beginning in AD330 when the centre of the Roman Empire moved from Rome to Byzantium (later Constantinople and now Istanbul), which lasted until the early 1400s. Byzantine refers to the architecture of the Byzantine Empire, with particular reference to pre-1400 non-Muslim architecture in Asia Minor, which is modern-day Turkey.

C Canali, Guido

A particularly important Italian architect of recent times who works primarily in and around Parma in northern Italy. He is a specialist in the restoration and reinvention of historic buildings, as well as exhibition design and museology (the study and science of designing museums). Canali carefully incorporates the requirements of historic buildings and works of art with the form of the existing and the new. In the early 1990s he also designed the interiors of two cruise ships.

Canali designed the Galleria Nazionale in Parma, Italy, in 1987. His development of an intelligent circulation route, using stairs, bridges, ramps and walkways, unites the complex of contrasting and discordant spaces, allowing the visitor to engage with both the building and the exhibits within.

C Cantilever

The process of extending a floor or other structural element beyond the existing walls of the building. The lack of any visible means of support gives this device a dramatic and slightly dangerous quality. Structural support is provided by tying the cantilevered elements back to the bulk of the rest of the building.

The required number of apartments for the Wozoco development, by MVRDV in Amsterdam, has been achieved by projecting rooms out of the building via a huge cantilever.

C Casson Mann

Casson Mann designed the Camouflage Exhibition at the Imperial War Museum, London, in 2007.

A British design office formed in 1984 by Dinah Casson and Roger Mann, who are well-known exhibition designers. Noted in Britain for their redesign of the 15 British Galleries at the Victoria and Albert Museum, London, they have also more recently redesigned the Churchill Museum in the Cabinet War Rooms. They have worked internationally, attracting controversial attention in the United States for their exhibition at the New York Museum of Sex in 2002.

C Ceiling

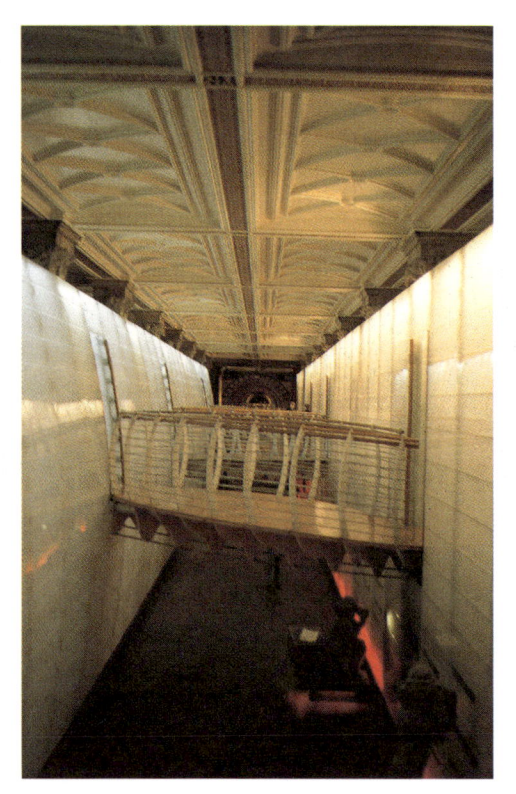

The ornate ceiling of the Natural History Museum in London, UK, is in stark contrast to the minimal walls of the newly installed Ecology Gallery.

The overhead plane of an internal space. The form of the ceiling will depend on its individual function, both aesthetically and practically. In baroque palaces the ceiling is often incredibly ornate, constructed from moulded plaster and then painted. In a modern office environment, on the other hand, the ceiling is often made of suspended tiles, which hide the servicing, wiring, air-conditioning ducts and lighting. In a domestic space, a ceiling is usually a flat surface painted white, which allows the light to reflect down and increase the level of light within a room.

☛ see Baroque 35, Domestic 77

C Chair

Perhaps the most recognisable form of furniture, the chair is traditionally one of the most important of the furnishing elements. It can serve as both a functional piece and an aesthetic feature. The chair is an item that has been constantly reinvented by many noted architects and interior designers; it is a form that is central to design and architecture.

The iconic Barcelona Chair, designed by Ludwig Mies van der Rohe for the German Pavilion at the Barcelona World Fair in 1929.

C Circulation 50

The space, object or act of movement within a building; it is the mechanism that provides movement from one part of the interior to another. Circulation elements and spaces include corridors, bridges, passages, elevators and staircases. Modes of circulation include vertical (via stairs and lifts) and horizontal (via corridors and bridges).

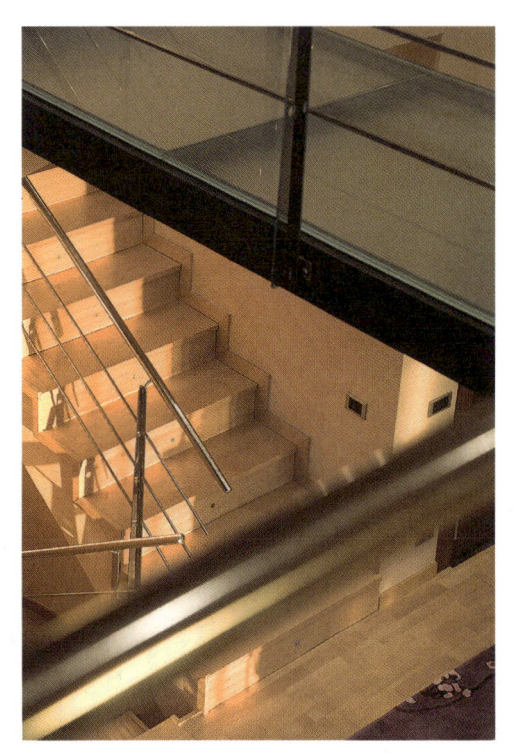

C Cladding 51

A material that is non-structural and is attached to the surface of a building, cladding may come in many forms and materials. For example, a concrete building may be clad in a more luxurious material and it is very common for steel- or concrete-framed buildings to be clad or 'faced' in marble or travertine. Redesigned buildings are commonly re-clad to give them a cosmetic facelift, so a tired old building may be re-clad in ceramic, stone or metal panels.

The local gneiss stone of Vals, Switzerland, is used to 'face' the concrete structure of the Thermal Baths, designed by Peter Zumthor.

C Classical 52

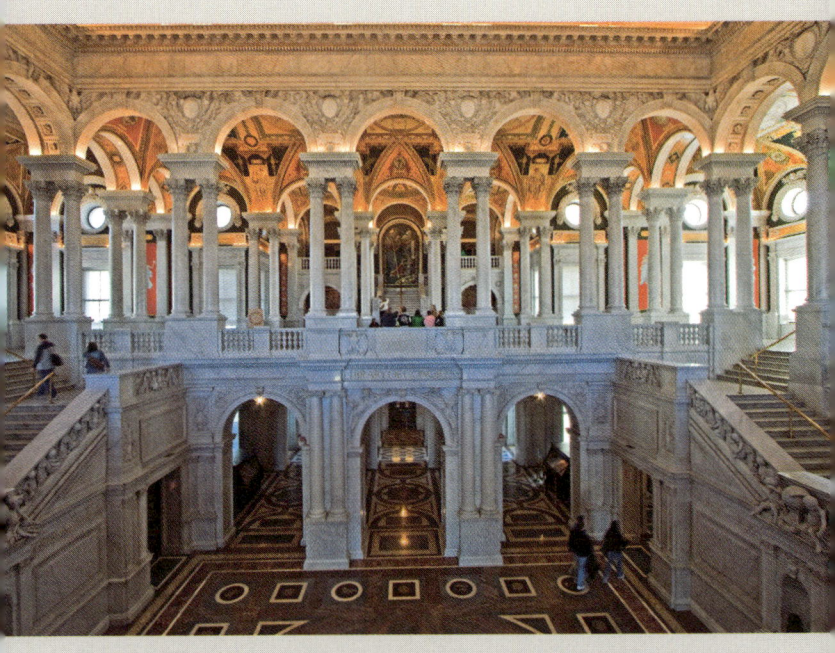

A style of architecture and design employed throughout the Western world. It is inspired by the architecture of ancient Greece and Rome and has its basis in the post and beam, or column, structural system. It is an architectural form widely employed in religious and governmental buildings, such as the Library of Congress in Washington DC, USA (pictured above). It alludes to the time of great power and civilisation that ancient Greece and Rome have come to represent in the Western world.

C Climate 53

Climate describes the particular environmental conditions within a specific area. The climate of an environment has a huge impact on the design of a building and invariably has to be controlled. This control of climate can be achieved in a variety of ways; most commonly this is done using artificial and energy-consuming air-conditioning systems. Other more passive or natural systems can be employed if designed into a structure early on. In the vernacular architecture of Asia and Africa, natural ventilation and use of particular materials is dictated by extreme climatic conditions.

In the Eden Project in Cornwall in the UK, the interior temperatures are regulated and controlled by the giant steel- and plastic-clad domes.

☛ see Ventilation 252, Vernacular 253

C Coates, Nigel

The Living Bridges Exhibition, designed by Nigel Coates, consisted of a series of models linked by a river, displayed in the main halls of the Royal Academy in London.

A British architect and interior designer who has worked for most of his early career in Japan. Famed for his outlandish postmodern designs, Coates is associated with avant-garde architecture. Some of his most notable work is in Tokyo, including the Metropole and Café Bongo. He is a well-published theorist of architecture and urban design; of particular note is his book *Ecstacity* in which he imagines a future city constructed from fluid forms and spaces.

☞ see Avant-Garde 32, Postmodernism 193

C Colombo, Joe 55

An Italian furniture and product designer whose short career produced some of the most innovative designs of the 1960s. Colombo (1930–1971) was a maverick who most notably created the first chair to be moulded from one material, a vacuum-forming stackable plastic chair that revolutionised the way people thought about furniture and materials. Colombo had a mission to 'furnish the habitat of the future'; his work embodied the zeitgeist of the 1960s.

Joe Colombo made futuristic interior spaces that consisted of unusual designs for everyday objects such as beds and tables. He often tested prototypes in his own home.

see Zeitgeist 270

C Colour

White
Purity, innocence, goodness and cleanliness.

Black
Magical, dramatic, elegant, sinister and sophisticated.

Gold
Wealth, extravagance, excess, luck and tradition.

Bright yellow
Hopeful, cheery, but also cowardly and deceitful.

Golden yellow
Sunny, autumnal, but also a warning.

Silver
Prestige, grandeur, value, cool and metallic.

Electric blue
Dynamic, engaging, bold and exhilarating.

Royal blue
Committed, dramatic, professional and vibrant.

Lime
Acidic, tart, refreshing, juicy and zestful.

Scarlet red
Exciting, dynamic, dramatic and aggressive.

Orange
Fun, glowing and vital, the warmest of colours.

Dusty pink
Romantic, luscious, tender and sentimental.

Colour is the property of an object that allows it to produce different sensations on the eye due to the way it reflects or emits light. Certain colours are considered to have physical properties and strong cultural associations. A few of these are shown here. The choice and interaction of colour is imperative to the designer as it can affect the way in which a space is experienced or perceived.

C Column

A vertical structural element that is used to support the deadweight of a roof or wall. Columns are commonly associated with the orders of classical architecture (as shown below), which are used according to the building's function, position and importance. Columns are also employed in modern buildings, where they can take on an entirely different identity, despite their identical structural properties.

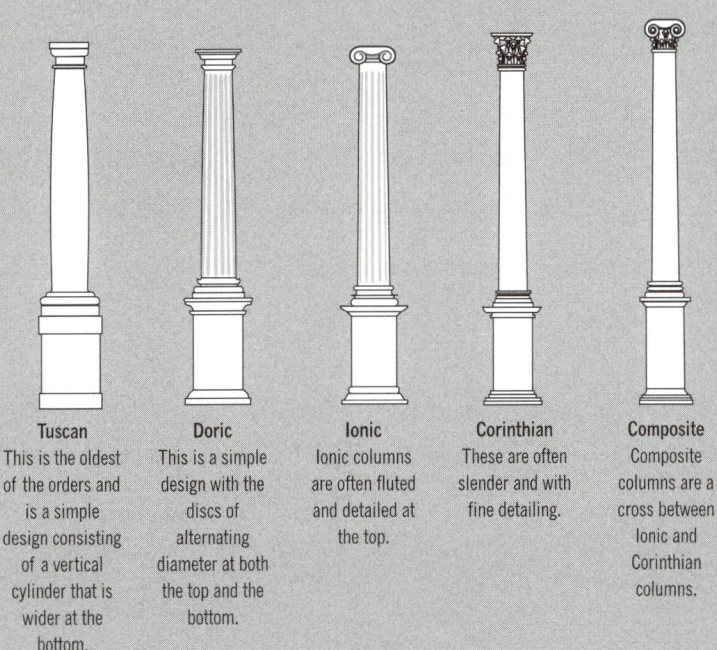

Tuscan
This is the oldest of the orders and is a simple design consisting of a vertical cylinder that is wider at the bottom.

Doric
This is a simple design with the discs of alternating diameter at both the top and the bottom.

Ionic
Ionic columns are often fluted and detailed at the top.

Corinthian
These are often slender and with fine detailing.

Composite
Composite columns are a cross between Ionic and Corinthian columns.

see Classical 52

C Conran, Terence 58

Famed for founding the Habitat furnishing store, Conran is one of the most popular and influential of a generation of British designers. Habitat revolutionised British buying trends by bringing modern interior furnishings to the notoriously conservative 1950s consumer. Habitat signalled the end of post-war austerity and the emergence of the 1960s consumer revolution. Conran went on to create a chain of restaurants and a more exclusive furnishing store, The Conran Shop.

see Retail Design 213

C Conservation

There are a number of different methods used in the conservation of a structure and there are distinct differences between each approach:

Preservation maintains the building in the found state.

Restoration is the process of returning the condition of the building to its original state.

Renovation is the practice of renewing and updating the building.

Remodelling or **adaptation** is the process of entirely altering a building.

Sometimes two or more of these methods may be employed in unison.

C Constructivism

Founded in 1913 by Vladimir Tatlin, constructivism has roots in many of the European proto-modernist movements, including cubism and Futurism. Constructivism was, like the modernist movements of Europe, based on the purity of the machine aesthetic. Constructivist work is notably geometric in form and was often produced through mathematics rather than artistic inspiration. The movement was initially supported by the Soviet Union after the 1918 Russian Revolution, but was eventually declared unsuitable for mass propaganda purposes.

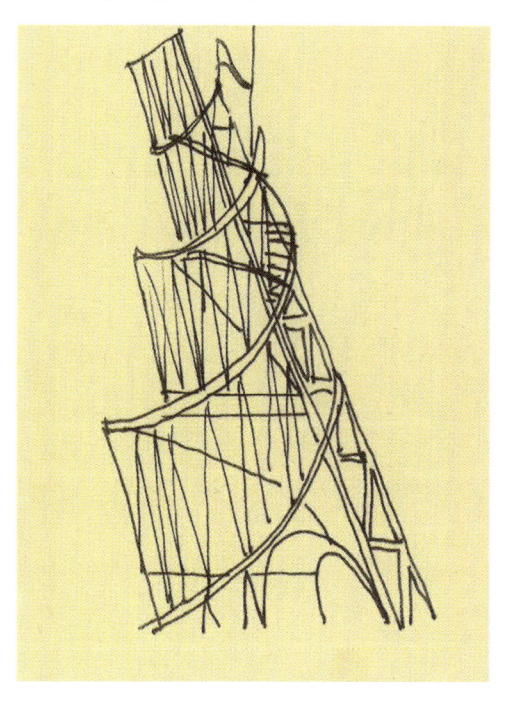

Tatlin's Tower is a poetic mixture of geometrics and mathematics with a revolutionary message.

see Geometry 115, Machine Aesthetic 155

C Context

The P.S.1 gallery in New York, pictured left, was once a school. Features such as staircases and corridors have retained the institutional feel of the space. The context has been exploited to add atmosphere to the gallery.

This is the environment or situation in which a design or object is placed or created. A context can be many things; in interior architecture it represents the physical environment in which a scheme is created (the existing building, for example). A building also has a broader context that is its place within its environment or urban setting. How the building fits into its context affects how any new interior might respond to the building. The term can also refer to the theoretical context of architecture and design.

C Cooling 62

The Minnaert Building in Utrecht is cooled by natural methods. Rainwater is collected inside the building and is filtered by trays of shellfish before being pumped through the building.

An aspect of environmental control, the cooling of space can be achieved in a variety of natural and artificial ways. One of the most common cooling methods used in the West is air-conditioning, where electronic air circulation units use chemical coolants to remove the heat from air and recycle it in a closed loop. Natural ventilation methods such as the stack effect are increasingly being used within buildings. This system utilises the natural flow of rising hot air to pull in cold air beneath it.

see Stack Effect 234, Ventilation 252

C Cornice

An aspect of classical architecture, the cornice consists of the cross-member or beam on top of a row of columns. As with much classical architecture, this beam is invariably ornamented and detailed. It also serves a structural purpose by spreading the weight of the wall, roof or portico equally across the load-bearing columns, thus ensuring a safe distribution of weight.

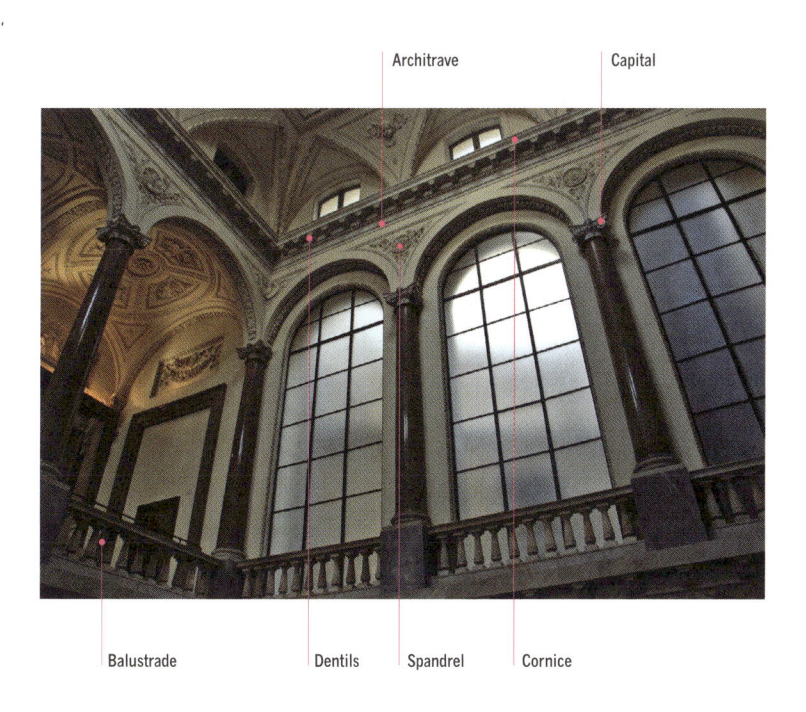

Architrave | Capital

Balustrade | Dentils | Spandrel | Cornice

see Classical 52, Column 57, Portico 191

C Corridor 64

As well as facilitating movement and joining spaces, corridors such as this one in Girona University, Spain, can become inspired spaces when animated by light.

The corridor is a linear space that connects a series of rooms. Corridors often feature in large public buildings such as offices, hospitals and schools, and are used to provide access to private rooms and other parts of buildings in the most efficient way possible.

see Circulation 50, Enfilade 90

C Counterpoint 65

A musical term used also in design to describe the aesthetic relationship between two opposing elements. In music it describes two voices that are different enough to be noticed but not to create disharmony. In design, the counterpoint refers to opposing or contrasting forms or spaces.

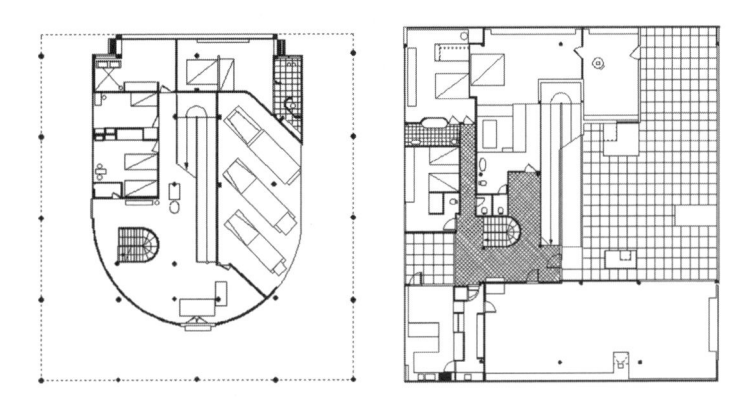

Ground-floor plan (above left) and first-floor plan (above right) of the Villa Savoye by Le Corbusier. Note the use of counterpoint in the organisation of the interior, where curved forms are placed in direct contrast with the orthogonal plan.

C Coving

A TRIM OR STRIP OF MATERIAL THAT MEDIATES THE JUNCTION BETWEEN THE TOP OF A WALL OR COLUMN AND THE INTERIOR CEILING. LIKE A SKIRTING BOARD, THIS IS LARGELY USED FOR DECORATIVE PURPOSES AND TO HIDE ANY UNTIDY JOINING OF MATERIALS. COVING IS DISTINCT FROM A CORNICE.

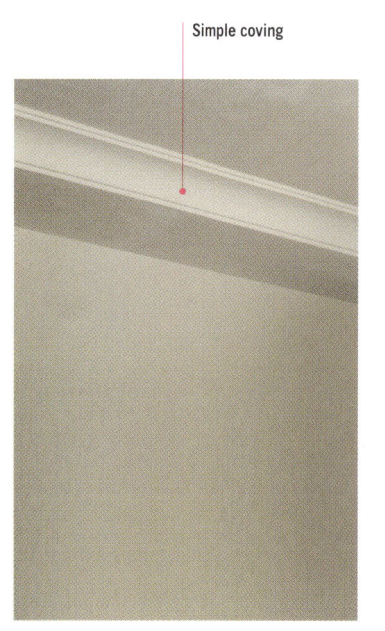

Simple coving

Decorative coving

see Column 57, Cornice 63, Skirting 229

Crawford, Ilse

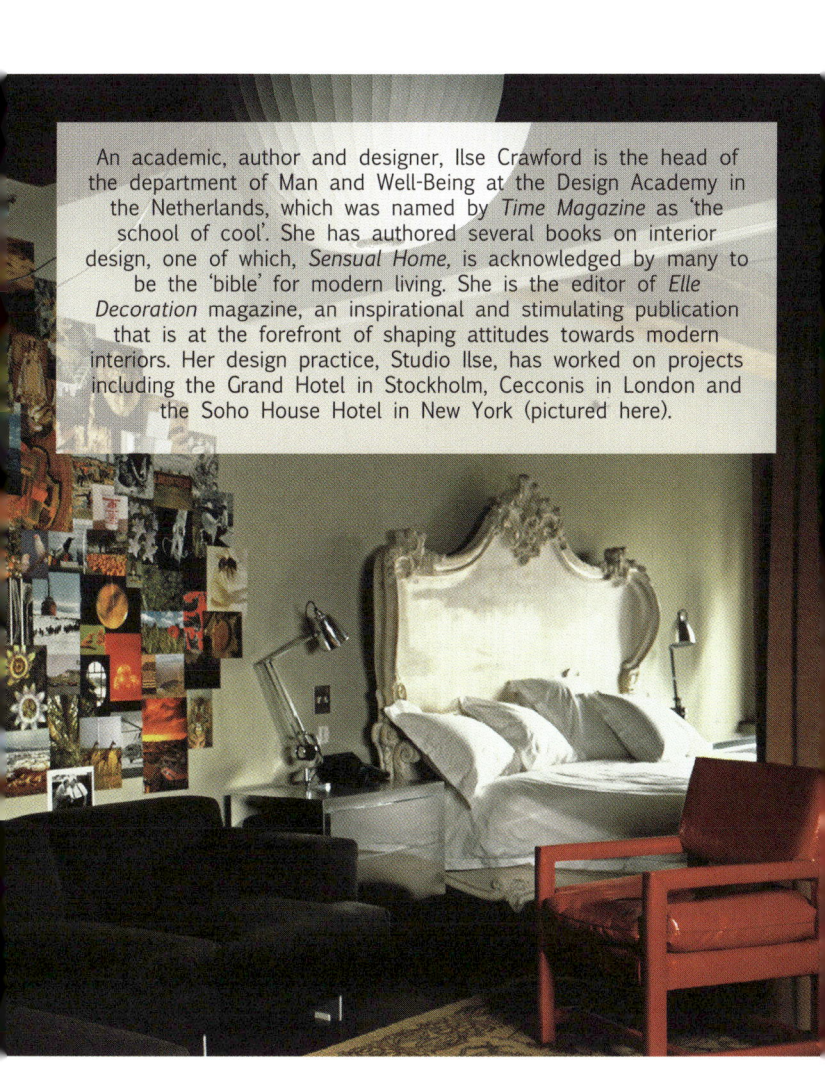

An academic, author and designer, Ilse Crawford is the head of the department of Man and Well-Being at the Design Academy in the Netherlands, which was named by *Time Magazine* as 'the school of cool'. She has authored several books on interior design, one of which, *Sensual Home,* is acknowledged by many to be the 'bible' for modern living. She is the editor of *Elle Decoration* magazine, an inspirational and stimulating publication that is at the forefront of shaping attitudes towards modern interiors. Her design practice, Studio Ilse, has worked on projects including the Grand Hotel in Stockholm, Cecconis in London and the Soho House Hotel in New York (pictured here).

C Curious Boym 68

Curious Boym is a furniture and product design company, formed in 1986 and named after the founding partner, Constantine Boym, and the American cartoon monkey, Curious George. Producing furniture and designing products for Alessi, Vitra and Swatch among others, Curious Boym works in all manner of mediums, including chain-link fencing and washing machines. The company has produced other more controversial projects and installations, such as a model of the Federal Building in Oklahoma City (shown here), from the 'Buildings of Disaster' series, which was designed to commemorate the loss of significant architectural landmarks.

see Alessi 19, Droog Design 82, Vitra 257

C Curtains

Curtains are one of the most recognisable elements of interior decoration. Primarily used to block views and prevent heat escaping through windows at night, they can also be used as a flexible temporary barrier in public buildings such as theatres. In certain domestic environments various materials and methods of decorating curtains have been used to communicate wealth and status; they can for instance be sumptuous and elaborate to create a room full of luxury and good taste. Illustrated below are just some of the terms associated with curtains and curtain making.

Fabrics
Thicker, heavier fabric tends to hang better.

Tie-backs
These can add colour and style to curtains and window dressings.

Eyelets
A method of hanging curtains without using pleats and hooks.

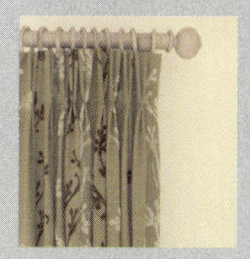

Heading
Shown here is a double pleat heading. Triple and French pleats can also be used.

Swags and tails
The swag decorates and hides the curtain pole, the tail drapes down the side.

Poles and finials
Curtains are secured on poles using finials, which can take virtually any shape.

D Deconstruction 70

Deconstruction originated as the literary process of dismantling a text to reveal the underlying message. Deconstructivists believe that language is inherently unstable and can be read in a number of different ways depending upon the position of both the author and the reader. It is a relatively new architectural movement and is based on the theories developed by the French philosopher, Jacques Derrida. Three-dimensional forms can be dismantled and separated into their constituent parts and then reassembled, based not upon custom, convention or tradition, but upon twenty-first-century needs.

The London Metropolitan University Graduate Centre building by Daniel Leibeskind is assembled from a series of irregular forms that relate to such contextual features as the North Star.

see Constructivism 60, Modernism 168-169

D Design

Design is a concept that relates to just about anything the human race has ever produced. Everything on some level has been designed, whether it is a table, a fork or a cathedral. Design is the process by which an idea becomes a drawing, which in turn becomes an object.

The design process is essentially a problem-solving procedure whereby the designer sets out to resolve the list of requirements into a physical object or space. The design process for interior designers might be divided into four stages:

Stage 1: Preliminary meetings and client brief

Stage 2: Surveys and building analysis, initial concepts and presentation to client, budget costings.

Stage 3: Working drawings, appointment of contractors, applications for consent, client estimates.

Stage 4: Project management and completion and handover of new interior.

D De Stijl 72

Founded by Theo van Doesburg in 1917, the Dutch movement De Stijl, which translates literally as 'the style', brought together artists, designers and architects. Gerrit Rietveld, who became De Stijl's best-known designer, is famed for his Red and Blue Chair (shown here), which is a seemingly abstract physical manifestation of a Piet Mondrian painting; red and blue planes with black and yellow structural members. Rietveld is also well known for the Schröder House, which consists of a series of intersecting planes that pass each other rather than joining at the edges.

☛ see Modernism 168–169, Painting 180

D Detail

Perhaps the most affecting aspect of a design is the detail; it is the intimate examination of the particular joints and materials. As the German modernist Ludwig Mies van der Rohe said: 'God is in the details'. Detail does not refer to complexity per se, but to intricacy. Attention to detail is one of the most important aspects of an interior, as it is often the aspect of a building with which the user has the most daily contact. The smallest details can enliven or bring meaning to mundane aspects of a space.

This bronze doorstop in the Brion-Vega Cemetery in Possagno, Italy, is designed by Carlo Scarpa. It ensures that the chapel door does not slide too far back into the space.

see Modernism 168–169, Mies van der Rohe, Ludwig 164

D Diller Scofidio + Renfro 74

An American design practice formed in 1979 by husband-and-wife team Elizabeth Diller and Ricardo Scofidio. Their work is interdisciplinary, ranging from objects and installations to performances and electronic media, all of which are utilised in their architecture. They have produced buildings that could be described as permanent installation art rather than structures. Their work has expanded recently into urban-scale projects with the support of new partner, Charles Renfro. Pictured is the Brasserie restaurant, which is placed in the basement of the infamous modernist classic Seagram Building in New York.

see Installation 129

D Disability Legislation

Many countries now require that public buildings be planned in accordance with a regulatory framework that ensures accessibility for all people. Amongst other things, disability legislation might require that architectural designs meet minimum and maximum requirements on doorway widths, step sizes, handrail heights and the length and gradient of ramps. Such regulations aim to enable independent access for all.

D Dome

A dome is a structural element conventionally used to cover large spaces. It is defined as an arch that has been rotated around its vertical axis. The dome, which has its beginnings in classical architecture, symbolises the vault of heaven and features widely in religious architecture. A recent example is Norman Foster's glass dome atop the redeveloped Reichstag in Berlin (shown here), which forms part of the public space and gives the visitor the opportunity to look down on their elected representatives while also giving panoramic views of the city.

see Arch 22

D Domestic

A term used in interior design to describe domestic buildings and anything designed for the home. Domestic design comes in many forms, from the collapsible yurts of the nomadic tribesmen of Mongolia, to mass-produced Victorian terraced houses. Domestic design and domesticity is a subject with considerable intellectual theory underpinning it, although it is often questionable whether contemporary house builders are aware of this.

D Donald, Stephen

The senior partner of sda, Donald has worked on a range of projects from large-scale, new-build social housing to small retail outlets. The majority of sda's work (and that for which it has gained its reputation) is in the design of music venues and bars. sda is noted for its work with existing buildings; it has developed a methodology, self-named 'resuscitation'. This refers to the remodelling of a building when it or its use has become obsolete. Shown here is the counter of Donald's Camden Ticket Shop in London, England.

D Door 79

An element that occupies an opening in a wall to allow access to a building or room within a building. Doors are usually placed at the threshold of a building and so form the moment of change from inside to outside, or from dark to light.

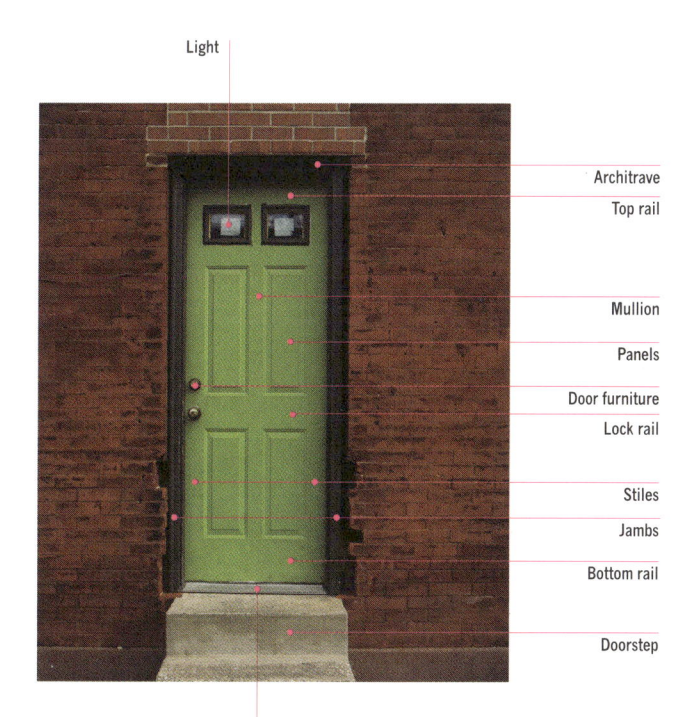

- Light
- Architrave
- Top rail
- Mullion
- Panels
- Door furniture
- Lock rail
- Stiles
- Jambs
- Bottom rail
- Doorstep
- Sill

D Drainage

A system used to dispose of used water effectively. On the exterior of buildings, rainwater needs to be drained away from the building in order to prevent flooding and structural damage, so drainpipes, gutters and soakaways are used. Internally, kitchens and bathrooms require drains with wastepipes to ensure polluted waste water is disposed of into sewers. 'Grey water' from rainwater, sinks, baths and washing machines can be recycled for other activities, such as in toilets or on the garden. 'Black water' from the toilet cannot be reused.

The plumbing in the bathroom of the home and office of Randy Brown Architects in Omaha, Nebraska, USA, makes a dramatic statement. It is artfully exposed, elevating its utilitarian function to that of a sculpture within the room.

D Drawing 81

The skill of drawing is a vital part of the design process and is also the language by which designers communicate their ideas to others. Here are the types of drawings used by interior designers and architects:

A sketch is a quick, loose and open drawing. It can be categorised in the following ways: conceptual, which communicates the essence of the idea; analytical, which can be used to analyse a building, space or component; and observational, which can be used to describe aspects of a building, space and materials.

Three-dimensional images can create an impression of what it might be like to occupy a building and has the advantage of allowing adjustment of viewpoint. They can be combined with other two-dimensional drawings to give a convincing overall impression of a scheme or project.

Orthogonal drawings are made to scale and offer insight into the dimensional relationship between the parts and the whole. There are two principal types of orthographic drawings: sections (see page 225) and elevations (see page 89).

Layout and presentation aims to represent a future space to a client. Drawings such as plans, sections and elevations explain a building in a measured and defined form. These types of drawing can tell a story in a considered and coherent way.

D Droog Design

Droog interiors and furniture are surprising and unexpected. Note the oversized lampshades in the bar (top) and the radical *Chest of Drawers* (bottom).

A Dutch design collective formed in Amsterdam in 1993, Droog Design has produced some of the most original conceptual furniture of recent times. Working largely with found objects in an almost Duchamp-esque ready-made fashion, Droog member Tejo Remy produced *Chest of Drawers* in 1991; a pile of drawers from various pieces of furniture held together with a strap. Droog followed in the tradition of the Italian Memphis movement of the early 1980s by shaking up a very sober form of design that had developed in the late 1980s.

☛ see Duchamp, Marcel 83

D Duchamp, Marcel

The highly influential Franco-American artist (1887–1968) whose career was defined by his ready-mades (sculptures produced using found objects), which he created between 1913 and 1917. His famous work *Fountain* (1917) (shown here), was an upturned urinal that stunned the art world and turned Duchamp into an international celebrity overnight. The sculptures were considered to be art because Duchamp had placed them in an art gallery and proclaimed them to be so. This was a radical and dangerous idea and one that even today, almost 100 years later, is still controversial.

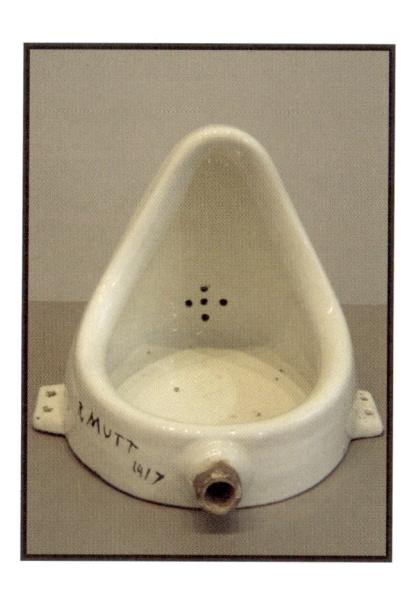

D Dwelling 84

A dwelling is a place of residence — a domestic environment or home. Pictured here is the interior of a yurt, the traditional dwelling of nomadic tribesmen of the Siberian Steppes of Russia and Mongolia.

E Eames, Charles and Ray

Charles and Ray Eames were an American husband-and-wife team who, along with John Entenza (editor of *Arts & Architecture* magazine) and other notable Californian architects, designed a series of steel-structured houses. This was an attempt to establish a cheap-housing type for the southern Californian climate. The couple are also remembered for the range of furniture they produced. Pictured below is the Eames Chair that is famous for its 'Eiffel Tower' stands. The Eameses are revered as being two of the most influential American designers of the twentieth century.

E Edge

86

The floor edge (pictured) in the Town Hall in Hillversum, Holland, by Dudok, is clearly delineated as the junction where one material ends and another begins. Note the highly reflective deep skirting.

The end of a surface or the border between two surfaces. It is the point at which a change in direction or material takes place on a surface. The edge of a surface or element can be used to direct the user visually or physically through the space. The edge may also be used to provoke a response from the occupant, with perhaps a sudden or discordant change in the nature or colour of the material. It is also a term coined by the urban theorist, Kevin Lynch, to describe the border between one district and another within a city.

E Edwardian

A period of British history dating 1901–1910 and defined by the reign of Edward VII (although culturally, it extended to the outbreak of the First World War in 1914). It was a time of sober reflection on the decorative excesses of Victorian design and architecture; it was also the period when a long-time king-in-waiting was finally able to realise his many plans for the improvement of society. Much of the best-regarded domestic architecture and urban planning in Britain was either built or conceived during this period.

The Edwardian terrace interior is characterised by sober decoration, which was typical of this period.

see Domestic 77, Victorian 254

E Element

88

An element can be used to totally reinvent a space. In Haus im Haus by Behnisch Architekten, the newly inserted six-storey house has been implemented into the old Chamber of Commerce building in Hamburg, Germany. The house within the building is the element that enlivens the old building, providing modern elegance, which casts a new light on a historical setting.

Element describes both an object in space and an aspect of a larger whole. In interior architecture, an element can be a complete new interior or an inserted object within a structure. Such insertions are used to totally reinvent the space, describing the new use visually. An element can also be part of a building: structural elements such as posts, beams, A-frames and columns, for example.

☛ see Column 57, Insertion 128, Structure 237

E Elevation

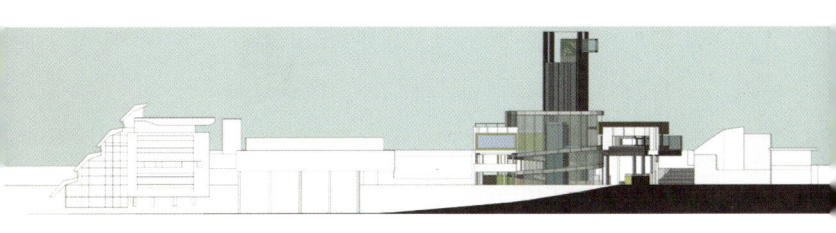

89

The term given to the view of a wall or façade of a building. When drawing the design of a building or interior, an elevation is used to show the whole of a building's façade in one diagram. This is not usually a view experienced in three dimensions, as an elevation is devoid of perspective or viewpoints and renders the façade in only two dimensions. Elevational drawings can be of the exterior or the interior.

☛ see Drawing 81, Façade 99

E Enfilade 90

A SERIES OF ROOMS LINKED TOGETHER WITHOUT THE USE OF A CORRIDOR OR OTHER CIRCULATION SPACE. THIS WAS THE NORMAL SPATIAL ARRANGEMENT WITHIN ALL BUILDINGS BEFORE THE SEVENTEENTH CENTURY AND IS NOWADAYS PARTICULARLY NOTICEABLE IN PICTURE GALLERIES ESTABLISHED IN EUROPEAN STATELY HOMES. THIS FORM IS STILL THE NORMAL ARRANGEMENT OF SPACES IN MOST MUSEUMS AND GALLERIES.

The enfilade arrangement of the rooms in the Dulwich Picture Gallery, London.

☞ see Circulation 50

E Engineering: Civil

One of the professional engineering disciplines, civil engineering concerns itself with the design and construction of certain aspects of the built environment, such as bridges, railways, roads and canals. Civil engineering was so-called to differentiate it from military engineering, which was previously the only form of engineering.

Construction of bridges such as the Tyne Bridge in Newcastle upon Tyne, UK, falls under the remit of civil engineering.

E Engineering: Electrical

One of the professional engineering disciplines, electrical engineering concerns itself with the design, installation and construction of the electrical systems used in structures. In domestic environments this will be basic wiring, or on an industrial scale, neon signs and street lighting.

The bright lights of Las Vegas – a tour de force of theatrical electrical engineering.

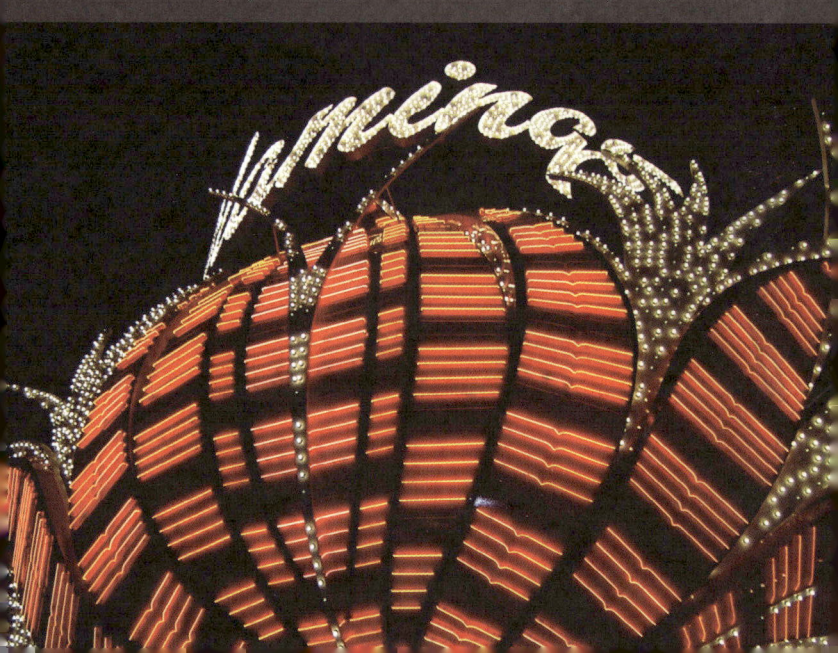

E Engineering: Mechanical 93

One of the professional engineering disciplines, mechanical engineering concerns itself with the design, installation and construction of the mechanical systems used in structures. From environmental control systems such as heating and cooling, to circulation systems such as lifts and escalators, mechanical engineering deals with all the machines that are used in our structures.

The Lloyd's Building, London, is turned inside out and its mechanical services such as lifts and toilets are external, allowing them to be easily changed when considered redundant.

☞ see Circulation 50

E Engineering: Structural 94

One of the professional engineering disciplines, structural engineering concerns itself with the design and construction of the structure of buildings and the elements in a building that make it stand up. Whether this is a steel or concrete frame or a solid stone wall, structural engineering ensures that the correct materials and specifications are used to make a building structurally sound so that it will not collapse.

The iconic Eiffel Tower is an elegant matrix of load-bearing structural elements, each calculated to withstand particular weights and forces and arranged to look beautiful.

see Element 88, Structure 237

E Environmental Control

The collection of processes, elements and machines that regulate the interior environment of buildings. These aspects include heating, cooling, drainage and air-conditioning systems. All these factors can be controlled naturally through the use of materials, the arrangement of external and internal spaces and the placement of openings. This is the most common method used in vernacular architecture. However, as building techniques have moved away from the vernacular, technological solutions have replaced the natural means of environmental control: air-conditioning, sun-tracking louvres and central heating systems are all artificial solutions to natural problems.

The services of the Pompidou Centre in Paris are exposed, allowing them to be exchanged when redundant and also giving the building a unique identity in the city.

☛ see Cooling 62, Drainage 80, Heating 122

E Ergonomics

The science and study of the relationship between people and their environment. A tool that is ergonomically designed will allow a person to use it with minimum effort and maximum comfort. It will be immediately apparent how to use an item that has been ergonomically well designed. For instance, we are all aware of how to use a hammer; it is evident from its design which part to hold and which part to use to hit the nail.

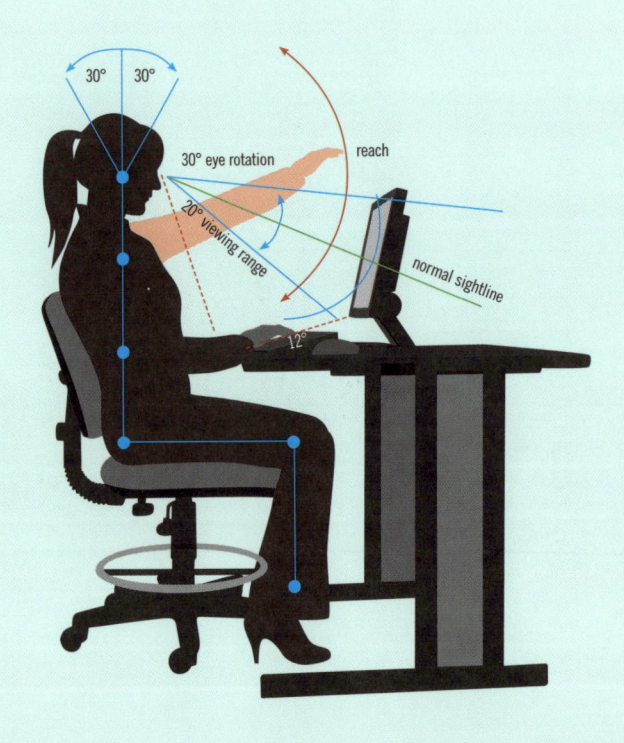

The relationship of a person to the objects that they use is an important consideration for the interior designer.

E Ethics

A set of moral principles that relate to or affirm a specified group, field or form of conduct. From the Greek *ethike*, which translates as 'the science of morals'.

Ethics, in Western philosophy, can be broadly divided into three schools of thought:

The first, drawn from Aristotle, holds that virtues (such as justice or charity) are dispositions to act in ways that benefit both the person possessing them and that person's society.

The second, defended by Kant, makes duty central to morality: humans are bound, from knowledge of their duty as rational beings, to obey the categorical imperative to respect other rational beings.

Thirdly, utilitarianism asserts that the guiding principle of conduct should be the greatest happiness or benefit of the greatest number.

E Exhibition Design 98

An aspect of spatial and interior design, exhibition design is a profession within a profession that concerns itself primarily with the design of temporary installations. Unlike the structural elements of an interior, the design of an exhibition is by its very nature transient. Exhibition design may be the travelling prefabricated stands used at trade shows and conferences (designed to be erected quickly and easily without expert help) or may be the more permanent and precious displays in a museum or art gallery.

Land Design Studio designed two of the four original exhibition spaces at Urbis in Manchester, England.

see Casson Mann 47, Land Design Studio 144

F Façade

The term used to describe the front wall of a building, the façade is the face the building shows to the world. The literal translation from the French word is frontage.
The façade is, at least in classical architecture, highly decorative, acting as a showpiece, presenting an ostentatious image of a structure. It is the first part of the building that communicates with the viewer and is therefore designed to be viewed.

The Petra Great Temple façade in Jordan is carved from the rock face and is an ostentatious demonstration of structure and proportion.

☛ see Classical 52

F FAT

Established in 1995, this British design practice is run by Charles Holland, Sean Griffiths and Sam Jacob. FAT (Fashion Architecture Taste) has produced some significant interior design projects and art-based projects early in its career. It has recently expanded into larger architectural and urban-scale regeneration projects in the UK. Its social housing projects have been described as leaning toward vernacular and its work is a critique on some of the more functionalist excesses of modernism.

Inside a former art gallery, FAT have created a unique and colourful office space that is organised into two pavilions placed around a 'public square'.

☛ see Vernacular 253, Modernism 168–169

F Floor

The surface in a building upon which one walks. In domestic or interior environments, the upper levels are invariably made from timber rafters and boards. Within an industrial or heavily trafficked space, a floor will be made from a hard-wearing material such as concrete or stone. Floors can also perform structural functions, such as holding a building together by bracing the walls.

The new stone floor of the Castelvecchio Museum in Verona, Italy, is laid with sufficient space at its edges in order to distinguish it from the old stone walls of the gallery.

see Ceiling 48, Wall 259

F Floor Covering

A generic term that describes all manner of materials and methods used to cover the floor of a space. The type of floor covering used in an interior is largely dictated by the function of the space. For example, kitchens and bathrooms almost invariably use hard waterproof coverings such as linoleum or ceramic tiles, while more domestic spaces employ softer, more comfortable coverings such as carpeting.

see Domestic 77

F Form

Form describes the basic shape of any element. Some objects will immediately lend themselves to a specific form; a table, for example, has to be of a certain form in order for it to fulfil its function as a raised horizontal surface to put things on. The form of an object, both inside and outside, can dictate people's reactions to it and its ability to perform a task.

The exterior form of a building will impose itself on the interior and thereby dictate the form and nature of those interior spaces.

The fluid exterior of Future Systems' Selfridges in Birmingham, UK (pictured right) is a powerful form that has a significant impact on the interior of the building (pictured above) as well the surrounding urban context.

F Formalism 104

Formalism regards the most important aspect of an object, building or space as its aesthetic quality. This design philosophy proposes that the appearance of an object is of the utmost importance; the consideration of the aesthetics is greater than the reasons for its existence, overriding any practical problems – even if it is incapable of being used as intended.

Frank Gehry's Guggenheim Museum in Bilbao is considered an object whose aesthetic quality is of the utmost importance.

see Narrative 173, Postmodernism 193

F Form Follows Form

An idea developed by Rodolfo Machado in an article that featured in the American journal *Progressive Architecture* in November 1976. Here Machado used the phrase 'form/form relationship' to introduce a new approach to the relationships between old and new. This approach is based on the idea that the form of the new elements of design are based on the form of the existing building, rather than being based upon functional requirements.

☞ see Form 103

Form Follows Function

A phrase first used in the late nineteenth century and associated with the American architect Louis Henri Sullivan, 'form forever follows function' came to embody the philosophy of the modern movement. Its central message is that the form or shape of an object or building is dictated by its function, not by an arbitrary idea of what it could or should look like. The beauty of an object is inherent in the way it is used. For example, it is found within the structural problems of making a building stand up, how it resists the weather, and its function.

☛ see Modernism 168–169, Le Corbusier 145

F Found Texture   107

The texture, surface or material from which an existing building is constructed can be described as 'found'. A fixture, fitting or surface that remains from the previous function of the building may be incorporated into the design of the new interior and will reveal the existing building's intrinsic worth, while making a connection between the past and present.

The graffiti left by Russian soldiers has been exposed and left as part of the remodelling of the Reichstag in Berlin, as a reminder of the turbulent history of the building.

see Surface 238, Texture 244

F Framing

108

The structural frame that supports a building; also the act of framing spaces and views through a building. Framing has a number of meanings: it is a common tactic used within architectural promenade, when a series of spaces are set up to allow a view to be framed from one specific point. It enhances a space and draws attention to an aspect of the design that is of particular importance.

The view out of a window at the Monastery of La Tourette in France, by Le Corbusier, is part of a carefully orchestrated sequence of framed views.

▶ see Architectural Promenade 24, Structure 237

F Free Plan 109

One of Le Corbusier's celebrated five points of architecture, the system by which he believed all architecture should and could be designed. The free plan was a direct consequence of another aspect of the five points, the piloti or columns. These columns support the structural load of the building, thus leaving the interior free. All walls, both external and internal, are non-load bearing and can therefore be placed anywhere and moved at will without affecting the structural integrity of the building.

The structural frame of Le Corbusier's Domino House exemplified the second of his five points of architecture: by using pilotis to support the structural load of the building, non-load-bearing walls could be used both internally and externally, thus freeing up the interior space.

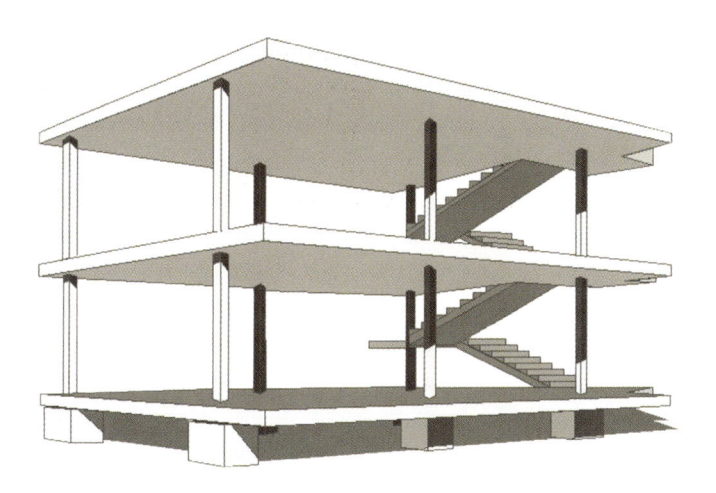

☞ see Le Corbusier 145, Load Bearing 150, Piloti 187

F Fresco

The Italian for fresh plaster, fresco is a particularly durable method of wall painting, using watercolours and precious metals on wet plaster. Some of the world's most famous works of art are frescos, such as Michelangelo's ceiling of the Sistine Chapel in the Vatican. Frescos were often used to tell Biblical stories to the largely illiterate congregations or to celebrate stories of the past, as shown in St Mark's Basilica in Venice, Italy (pictured above).

F Frieze

A feature of classical architecture, the frieze is used to decorate the porticos and pediments of a building. Running around the top of a wall above the cornice and below the pediment, the frieze invariably depicts the story of a battle or the lives of emperors. One of the most controversial and famous friezes is the Parthenon Marbles (pictured below), which were removed by British collector Lord Elgin from the temple in Greece in the nineteenth century, in order to prevent further damage to them.

see Classical 52, Cornice 63, Portico 191

F Function   112

A term used to describe the purpose or use of a space. The function of a space or building will define its design parameters. For example, an industrial space will not be designed in the same way as a domestic living room. The varying functions of interior spaces include living, eating, cooking, working, learning (as shown above), leisure, industry and circulation.

☞ see Room 217

F Furniture 113

This can vary from the obvious: chairs, tables, beds, wardrobes and sofas, to the less obvious: radiators, kitchen units, fireplaces and closets – even door furniture. Furniture can also take the form of elements that occupy the space or enclosed spaces. Furniture can be fixed or free; fixed furniture can be used in place of walls, to divide or determine spaces and their functions. Kitchen units used as furniture will determine the function of the space around them.

☛ see Chair 49, De Stijl 72, Product Design 197, Vitra 257

G Gensler

Gensler is a multi-disciplined global design practice whose interior experience and expertise has ensured a diverse selection of commissions, from packaging to the redesign of Shanghai docks. Gensler has also collaborated with other notable architects including Japanese firms SANAA and Shigeru Ban as well as Foster + Partners.

Gensler is particularly well known for its contemporary and dynamic approach – a prime example being the redesign of the London Stock Exchange (pictured above), which featured a moving sculpture in which suspended balls move up and down to reflect market shifts.

G Geometry   115

From the Greek *geometria* (*geo* = earth, *metria* = measure), geometry is a branch of mathematics concerned with size, form and the relative position of objects and properties of space. In a mathematical sense, it is most commonly encountered when talking of shapes – squares, triangles, tetrahedra, spheres – and how they relate to each other and to themselves. Similarly in buildings, it is the interrelationship of different forms or shapes. The juxtaposition of wildly differing forms can create dynamism in a building.

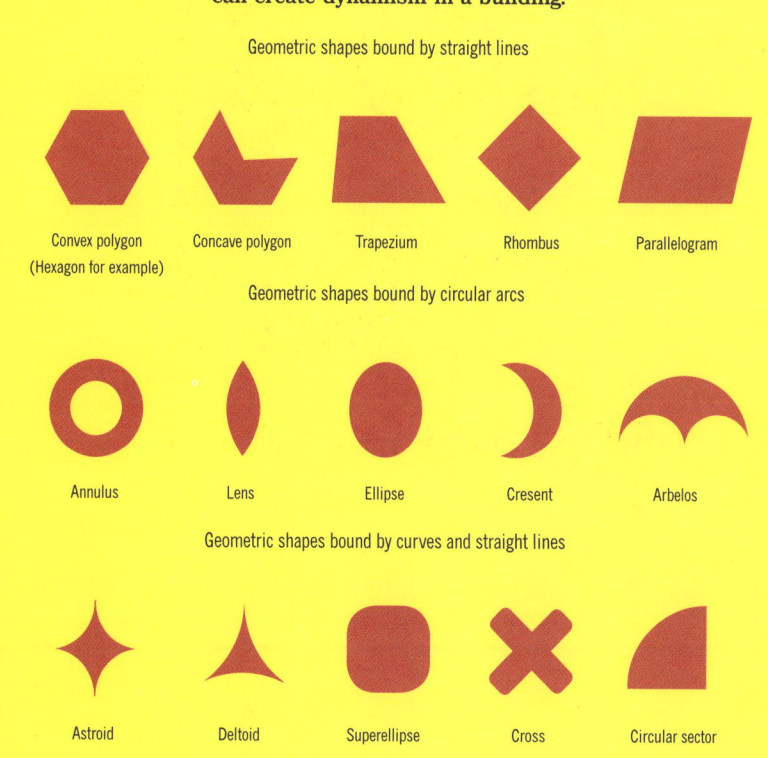

Geometric shapes bound by straight lines

Convex polygon (Hexagon for example)   Concave polygon   Trapezium   Rhombus   Parallelogram

Geometric shapes bound by circular arcs

Annulus   Lens   Ellipse   Cresent   Arbelos

Geometric shapes bound by curves and straight lines

Astroid   Deltoid   Superellipse   Cross   Circular sector

☛ see Art Deco 27, Bauhaus 36, Form 103

G Gesamtkunstwerk 116

A German word, which loosely translates as 'the complete artwork', gesamtkunstwerk, when applied to architecture and spatial design, describes a project that is designed as a cohesive whole, from the building itself to the smallest detail of the interior design. Charles Rennie Mackintosh applied this attention to detail in his design of the library at the Glasgow School of Art in Scotland (pictured here).

see Domestic 77, Scheme 224

G Golden Section   117

Also called the golden ratio, the golden section is approximately 1.618, or 5:8 expressed as a ratio. Since the Renaissance, and perhaps from as far back as ancient Greece, architects have used the golden ratio as a proportional system in the form of the golden rectangle. Within this, the ratio of the long side to the short side is the golden ratio and is commonplace in architecture. Although this proportion is irrational, it is believed that these proportions are naturally aesthetically pleasing.

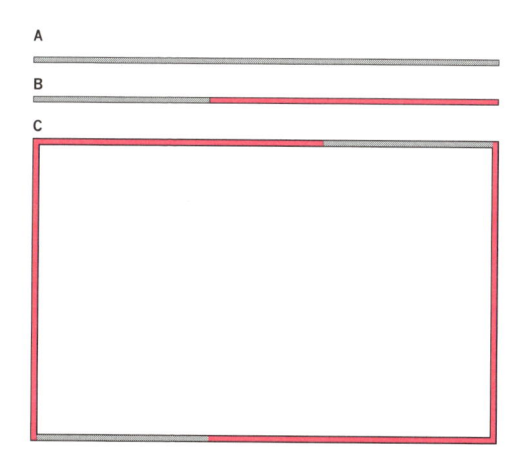

Much of Le Corbusier's architecture made reference to the golden section and other ancient proportioning systems.

A golden section can be constructed using a simple mathematical calculation:
Draw a line (A) and divide it by the ratio 8:13 (B).
The whole line (A) will form the long sides of the golden rectangle.
The longer segment of the dissected line (B) will form the shorter sides of the rectangle (C).

G Gothic Revival

A STYLE OF ARCHITECTURE PARTICULARLY POPULAR IN THE NINETEENTH-CENTURY. THIS STYLE WAS A REVIVAL OF GOTHIC ARCHITECTURE, WHICH HAD BEEN PRACTISED WIDELY IN CHURCH STRUCTURES BETWEEN THE TWELFTH AND SIXTEENTH CENTURIES. ONE OF THE KEY PROPONENTS OF THE GOTHIC REVIVAL IN BRITAIN WAS ARCHITECT AUGUSTUS PUGIN. THE GOTHIC REVIVAL ALSO CREATED THE ENVIRONMENT FROM WHICH THE ARTS AND CRAFTS MOVEMENT DEVELOPED IN THE LATTER PART OF THE CENTURY.

Illustrated is the Gothic revival interior of the House of Commons Chamber in London, UK.

see Arts and Crafts 29

G Graphic Design

The branch of design concerned with the creation of two-dimensional images and text. Graphic design is most commonly used in advertising, but also includes book and magazine design and packaging. Graphic design has gone from being a tool of advertisers to a form of art in its own right. Artists such as Roy Lichtenstein and Andy Warhol took the graphic design of products and magazines and turned it into art during the pop art period of the 1960s.

The interior of the Museum of Childhood in Bethnal Green, London (pictured) by Caruso St John playfully uses street signs to direct visitors to the various parts of the museum.

G Gray, Eileen

Largely overlooked during the early twentieth century as a lone female in a sea of male designers, Gray (1878–1976) was rediscovered in the late twentieth century. Unlike other prominent female designers of the age, such as Charlotte Perriand, she did not work with a male mentor. She gained recognition for her exhibit at the Paris Salon d'Automne in 1923, where Le Corbusier praised her work. Joe Colombo and Le Corbusier himself cite her as an inspiration.

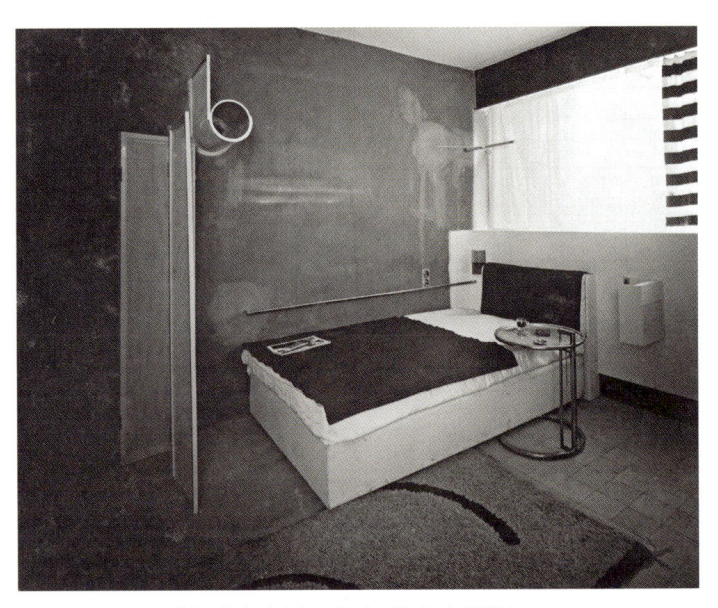

Pictured is Gray's bedroom interior of the iconic E-1207 house.

☛ see Colombo, Joe 55, Le Corbusier 145

G Guixé, Martí

A Spanish designer working in his native hometown of Barcelona and also in Berlin, Guixé designs products for shoemaker Camper as well as developing conceptual projects. He describes himself as a 'product designer who hates objects', even though he designs three-dimensional objects. He began his work for Camper in 1998, designing their London stores, and the relationship has since developed. Guixé's anti-materialistic attitude shows in his slogan on the Camper bag: 'If you don't need it, don't buy it'.

The Camper shop displays the footwear in a fun and irreverent manner with shoes stacked upon a tabletop supported by shoe boxes.

H Heating 122

Heating can be achieved by artificial and natural or 'passive' means. It is most commonly seen as central heating, consisting of a central boiler that heats water that is then pumped around metal radiators to emit heat to warm the space. Traditionally, rooms would be heated using wood- or coal-burning fires or in more primitive times a central fire in one large space. Heating can also be passive, utilising the power of the sun, whereby thick earth or stone walls absorb heat during the day and release it at night.

A series of elegant steel heating ducts punctuate the interior of the main banking hall of the Post Office building in Vienna.

G Hejduk, John

A graduate of the Cooper Union School of Art and Harvard, John Hejduk (1929–2000) was one of the most thoughtful and esoteric of modern American architecture theorists. He was a member of the New York Five, a think tank of influential American super-modern architects, along with Michael Graves, Charles Gwathmey, Peter Eisenman and Richard Meier. He is considered to have transformed architectural thinking, both practical and critical, at the Cooper Union. Hejduk's work was largely confined to models and paper.

One of the few works by Hejduk to be realised was the 'Clock/Collapse of Time', Bedford Square, London, 1986. Hejduk said: 'The clock tower moves through spatial time, elevational, flat time (90 degrees), then angular, isometric time (45 degrees), finally horizontal, perspective time (0 degrees)'.

see Modernism 168–169

H Hierarchy

When used in the context of design or architecture, hierarchy is concerned with the interrelationship of spaces. Within an interior, some spaces will always take precedence over others. For example, in a parliament the debating chamber will take precedence over the ancillary spaces that are subservient to it. There may also be a hierarchy of movement through a building, whereby certain routes, passages or stairs are the principal paths of communication through a space, with other routes being secondary. In City Hall in London (pictured above), for example, visitors can view the debating chamber as they ascend the spiral ramp to the top of the building, establishing a hierarchical relationship between view and movement.

see Space 233

H History   125

The history of a building, space or city is central to the process of interior architecture and design. In the reuse of existing buildings, a respect for and understanding of the history of a place is vital. The history should, in a good design, generate and shape the process of redesign, not hinder or obstruct it. Using the historical importance of a building or location to inspire a design will help to develop a thoughtful yet imaginative reuse.

The entrance to the Basilica in St Mark's Square, Venice, is distinguished by a series of different columns appropriated from different places over time.

☛ see Context 61, Reuse 214, Space 233

H Holl, Steven

Steven Holl has produced a number of notable buildings and has received numerous awards, including the 1998 Alvar Aalto Medal. He is considered to be a phenomenological architect, concerning himself with the concept of 'being' and how a person engages with their surroundings in an existential sense. He considers how meaning is assigned to an environment and how this meaning may not be embodied in the environment but merely in our perceptions of it. This idea of the user psychologically relating to an environment is vital in spatial design, for the character and qualities of a space are central to its success as a place. Pictured below is Holl's Storefront Gallery for Art and Architecture in downtown New York. Its façade breaks down the barriers between inside and outside.

H Hyper-Reality

A concept first discussed by the French philosopher Jean Baudrillard, hyper-reality is a seemingly 'super-real' depiction of something real. Baudrillard has argued that we live in a hyper-real world made up of signs, images and simulations that ignore objective reality. This idea has been referred to as the 'authentic fake'. Las Vegas in the USA (pictured above), typifies this notion, where a collection of inauthentic experiences of the world is created through mock buildings and landmarks. A stay here, for example, would result in a hyper-real experience.

I Insertion 128

The act of inserting an object or element into an existing building. An insertion is a bold tactic that will invariably and entirely change the existing building in line with its intended new use. The insertion may take the form of something drastic: a substantial portion of the existing building might be demolished and replaced with a new element. Or the insertion may take a more subtle form: it might involve the placement of a wall or other element that signals the new use.

A new doorway, neatly inserted into the old city wall that bisects the site of the Castelvecchio Museum in Verona, subtly links the two halves together.

☛ see Element 88, Tactics 241

I Installation   129

A site-specific form of art, installation art will always have a direct relationship to its surrounding physical context. Installation art generates or conveys meaning to a context but it invariably travels badly; when exhibited in galleries outside of its original context it can lose a substantial degree of meaning. Installations are like interior design: subsumed in context. The act of removing or ignoring that context leads to the diminishing of both. Pictured above is the Tourisms: suitCase Studies exhibition (1991) in the Whitney Museum, New York. The installation uses 52 suitcases to display information about each of the American states.

☞ see Context 61

I Interior Architecture 130

Interior architecture is concerned with the remodelling of existing buildings, attitudes towards existing spaces and structures and organisational principles. Interior architecture bridges the practices of interior design and architecture, often dealing with complex structural and environmental problems. This encompasses a huge range of project types, including theatres, museums, galleries and other public buildings. As a growing intellectual discipline, it is a subject that champions the reuse and reinvention of existing buildings. It engages with issues of conservation and sustainability, which have all become vital to the development of cities.

Carlo Scarpa's remodelling of the Revoltella Museum in Trieste, Italy symbolises all that interior architecture as an intellectual discipline advocates.

☛ see Interior Decoration 131, Interior Design 132

Interior Decoration

The practice of the adorning or decorating of an interior; it is principally a practice applied to environments that are not to be drastically changed, but made to appear visually different. Interior decoration confines itself to dressing a space in different materials and colours, and changing the furniture to create a new image. The use of materials is usually limited to fabrics, paints and small reversible interventions. Pictured above is Edward Prior's elaborately painted ceiling at St Andrews in Roker, near Sunderland in the UK.

☛ see Interior Architecture 130, Interior Design 132

Interior Design

The general term for any design concerned with the interior space. Interior design at one end of the spectrum may be labelled interior architecture, while at the other end it merges into the realm of the interior decorator. Interior design is often a misrepresented discipline, considered by many architects to involve only fixtures and furniture. It is therefore often consigned a less important role in the design of a building, even though it is central to the user's experience.

Ben Kelly is a hugely influential interior designer. Here we see his design of the entrance to the subterranean Gym Box in London.

see Interior Architecture 130, Interior Decoration 131

I Interior Education 133

Universities and colleges across the world provide formal academic programmes that lead to particular qualifications in an interiors-related subject.

These are generally categorised as undergraduate or postgraduate degrees.

In the UK these include Bachelor of the Arts (BA) and Master of the Arts (MA). In the USA the equivalent is classified as Bachelor of Fine Arts (BFA) and Master of Fine Arts (MFA). The PhD qualification, or doctorate, is recognised as one of the highest degrees that can be awarded.

In the UK interior education is represented by the group IE (Interior Educators).

An education in an interiors-related subject is key to a career in practice, and an aspiring designer should choose the course and the qualification that is appropriate to them.

see Qualification 201

I International Style 134

A name given to a period and a style of modernist architecture. The international style is identified as an aesthetic, principally featuring sheer planes of rendered white concrete, a free plan and the language of the machine. The international style was a term coined by American architects Henry-Russell Hitchcock and Philip Johnson, who were attempting to categorise the nature of modernist architecture.

The Lakeside Apartments in Chicago, USA, designed by Ludwig Mies van der Rohe, symbolise all that international modernism advocated.

see Free Plan 109, Modernism 168–169

I Intervention 135

A spatial manipulation designed to encourage an alternative way of using a space. The intervention may be a permanent reinvention or a temporary measure to purposely alter the way in which a space is used. Installation art can be described as an intervention as it results in the re-evaluation of the containing space. Similarly, a new opening or alteration to a façade intervenes with the existing to reveal or indicate the new. The intervention pictured here, entitled *Shibboleth* and designed by Doris Salcedo, involved creating a huge crack in the floor of the Turbine Hall in the Tate Modern, London. It represents the divisions that we currently see in the modern world.

see Installation 129, Space 233

J Jekyll, Gertrude

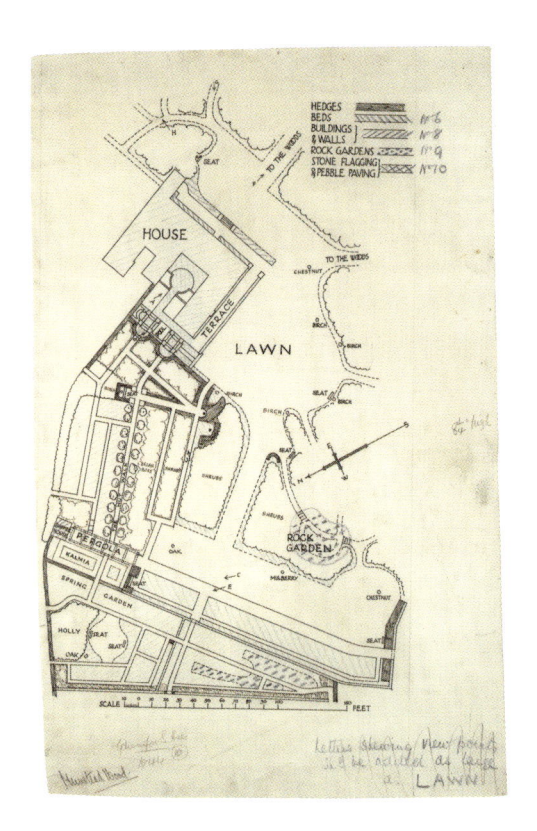

The British garden designer, writer and artist who created hundreds of gardens worldwide. Jekyll (1843–1932) was a collaborator of the English Arts and Crafts architect, Sir Edwin Lutyens, designing the landscapes and gardens for many of his projects. Jekyll had a painterly approach to her work and was unique in the profession of landscaping at the time; she considered colour and texture to be the most important aspects of a garden's design. Her colour theory was influenced by the Impressionists, in particular the English painter Turner. Pictured is the garden and house plan for Jekyll's own home at Munstead Wood in Surrey in the UK.

☞ see Arts and Crafts 29

J Jiřičná, Eva

Eva Jiřičná is famous for her glass and steel staircase. This one is in Browns Nightclub in London, UK.

Famed for her glass and steel staircases, Eva Jiřičná has worked extensively in the UK throughout her career. Jiřičná has worked with a number of well-known British architects as well as in her own right as an interior designer, particularly in the field of retail design. She brings an artistic and precious quality to her retail interiors, reinventing what is expected of a shop. The series of Joseph stores she designed in the late twentieth century were as well known for the tensile and sculptural staircases as they were for the clothes.

J Judd, Donald

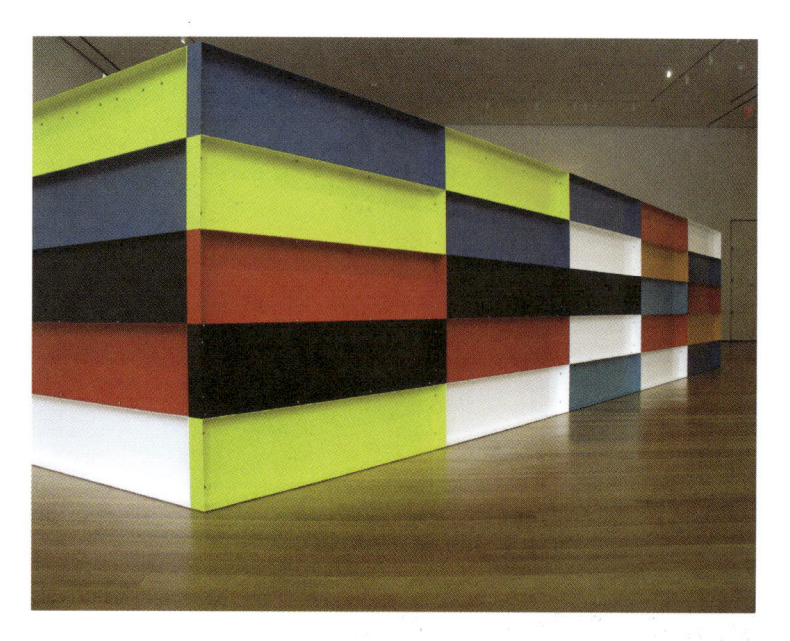

The American minimalist installation artist famed for his creation at the Museum of Modern Art in New York in 1964 (pictured above). The installation, an untitled row of boxes bolted together, caused a storm in the New York art scene in 1964. The work of Judd (1928–1994) is one of the best examples of how installation art can influence and create an interior environment. It affects the way we experience and relate to a space through the use of simple forms arranged and displayed in a rigorous manner.

☛ see Installation 129

Kelly, Ben

An English post-punk designer who made his name with a series of projects in Manchester for Factory Records: interior design for the Haçienda, Dry Bar and Factory Headquarters. His other projects include Bar Ten in Glasgow, the Children's Galleries at the Science Museum and the Design Council Offices. He is known for his use and manipulation of many different materials within a project and also for his use of ready-mades. Kelly describes interior design as something that has integrity far beyond just surface consideration and with its basis in the manipulation and control of space.

In this design for a Halfords store in Sheffield in the UK, Ben Kelly has reappropriated the 'ready-made' language of traffic bollards and hazard warning signs to become details of the interior.

K Klein Dytham Architecture

A practice formed by Astrid Klein and Mark Dytham in the 1990s in Tokyo. KDa put the individuality of their work down to the energy instilled in the practice by working in Japan. They identify with the Japanese thirst for the new and have a reverence for craftsmanship and careful use of materials. Their dual East–West perspective gives the practice an unconventional and different outlook.

KDa's Interactive Communication Experience (ICE) created for the lobby of Bloomberg's office in Tokyo, Japan. The screens respond to touch and movement, creating a kaleidoscope of light on the 80,000 pixel LED display.

K Klein, Yves

Klein is noted for his interior decoration and set work at the Gelsenkirchen Opera, Germany (1959). Pictured is a maquette of one of his stage designs, in the eponymous International Klein Blue.

A French artist who was one of the most influential of post-war Europe, Klein (1928–1962) has been classed by some as neo-Dada and was an early 'enigmatic' postmodern painter. His early post-war works are known as *Monochrome*, which is a series in black, white and grey. He later used a single shade of blue, which was identified as a new colour and was patented as International Klein Blue.

K Koolhaas, Rem

A Dutch graduate of the Architectural Association School of Architecture in London, Koolhaas is a prolific writer and theorist of contemporary architecture and also a practising designer and architect. While labelled a deconstructivist, he is perhaps the least pure of this school. Along with his architectural partner, Joshua Ramus (with whom he also set up the practice, Office for Metropolitan Architecture (OMA)), he is noted for his work on the Kunsthal in Rotterdam, Seattle Public Library and the Casa de Musica in Porto, shown in the picture below.

☞ see Deconstruction 70

Kroll, Lucien

The Belgian architect and academic, Lucien Kroll, is associated with forms of 'participatory architecture', in which the architect strives to enable the occupant to build their own building. In his most famous project, La Memé, Masion Médicale (pictured above), a student living quarter for the Catholic University of Louvain, Brussels (1969–1971), Kroll used a system whereby the final design was not fixed. All the internal walls were mounted on tracks in the floor and could be dismounted and reassembled in different configurations, creating a totally flexible and responsive interior that could be changed at will.

L Land Design Studio

Describing itself as a design consultancy rather than a practice, Land Design Studio was formed in 1992 by Peter Higgins. The studio describes its work as investigating 'how the creation of architectural space and interpretation of objects, people or corporate messages can be drawn together'. They are an interdisciplinary multimedia design firm and much of their work is in the areas of exhibition and gallery design. Pictured here is their design for the UK Pavilion at the 2005 Japan Expo. Here, they created an ambient atmosphere where visitors could discover British innovation.

L Le Corbusier

Le Corbusier – the *nom de plume* of the Franco-Swiss architect Charles-Edouard Jeanneret (1887–1965) – was one of the most prominent and influential practitioners of early twentieth-century European modernism. A prolific writer and architectural theorist, his best-known works are *Vers une Architecture* (1923) and *Le Modulor* (1948), which encapsulated the theory of modern architecture and scale. Le Corbusier's development of *Le Modulor* referenced the male form and a human scale, around which the proportions of modern architecture were developed.

Pictured is the fluid open space of the entrance hall in the Villa La Roche in Paris.

see Modernism 168–169

L Light: Artificial

Light is a vital component in any environment. The quality of light, especially artificial light, can entirely change the nature of a space. Artificial light is often employed to create mood; low-level lighting is used to generate an intimate environment, while coloured light can be used to give a space a certain ambience. In some cases artificial light is all that is available; in basements, for example, where no natural light can penetrate.

Carefully controlled coloured light animates the interior installation and guides visitors around the *Wonderful* exhibition, Wellcome Trust, London, by Ben Kelly Design.

see Colour 56, Space 233

L Light: Natural

Light pours in through the side wall of the Notre Dame du Haut chapel in Ronchamp, France, creating a serene and peaceful environment.

Natural light is a powerful phenomenon. In northern climes it is customary to make the most of natural lighting with the use of large windows. In hotter, brighter zones, windows are made smaller to block out direct light and heat. Natural light can, to a degree, be controlled, by shading that blocks, bounces or reflects it around a space to dramatic effect.

see Colour 56, Space 233

L Listed/Protected Buildings

Many countries now impose laws that are designed to protect certain buildings that are selected for architectural, historical or cultural value from demolition or significant alteration.

Protecting a building is a means of preserving the cultural heritage of a country and there are many protected structures worldwide that are considered by local authorities to be of special interest. Once a building is listed or protected, there is an obligation to preserve the protected structure.

In the UK the grades for the listed building scheme are as follows:

Grade I: These are buildings of exceptional interest (2 per cent of listed buildings).

Grade II*: These are particularly important buildings of more than special interest (4 per cent of listed buildings).

Grade II: These are buildings of special interest, which warrants every effort being made to preserve them.

☞ See Building and Planning Regulations 43

L Llewelyn-Bowen, Lawrence

A British daytime-television celebrity who led the vanguard that popularised interior decoration in the late 1990s. His most notable programme was *Changing Rooms* and the programme's commercial success provided a format that has been copied by various broadcasters in Britain and around the world. Although not interior architecture or design, these programmes have raised the profile of interior decoration as both a profession and a pastime. Llewelyn-Bowen has put his name to a large range of fabric and wallpaper designs, one of which is pictured here.

L Load Bearing 150

A term used to describe a wall or other element of a structure that supports its own weight and possibly that of other elements in a building. The masonry wall of a house can be considered load bearing as it supports the weight of the roof and the floors, that is, the rest of the building. Load-bearing structures can be constructed from many materials, including brick, stone and mud. Stone-made structures such as the castle pictured here have load-bearing walls, which are built up by layering stones so that the walls support their own weight and the weight of other elements within the building.

☞ see Element 88, Structure 237

L Loos, Adolf

An Austrian modernist who has become one of the most important architects of the period and the developer of Raumplan spatial organisation. These ideas were developed in the Müller House in Prague (1930) the Moller House in Vienna (1928) and the Tristan Tzara House, Paris (1927). Loos (1870–1933) was a major critic of the embellishment of pre-modern design, with particular reference to the work of the Viennese Secessionists. This critique culminated in the 1908 essay 'Ornament and Crime', a phrase that can be said to sum up the modernist philosophy. Pictured here is Adolf Loos' American Bar in Vienna. The compact quality of the space is alleviated by the mirrored walls, which suggest there is an infinite number of rooms beyond the one occupied.

see Modernism 168–169, Raumplan 206

L LOT-EK

152

A group of American architects who are one of the few who can lay claim to the overused term of blurring the boundaries between art and architecture. LOT-EK's work with found objects and everyday objects has successfully placed them in the avant-garde of architecture. They create novel solutions when using existing objects, creating unexpected spaces within and between their buildings. LOT-EK's past projects have stimulated debates about what constitutes architecture, in particular dwellings, and how we think about them as buildings.

LOT-EK's use of moveable cargo crates in The Bohen Foundation gallery allow the space to be reconfigured in a variety of ways.

see Avant-Garde 32

L Louvres 153

Derived from the French word *l'ouvert*, meaning 'the open', louvres consist of a series of slats held in a frame on the exterior of a building. They are angled to allow filtered light and air in but to keep direct sunlight out. Louvres are largely used in sunny climes but are increasingly being used in northern latitudes on glazed buildings, as part of an attempt to reduce solar gain in naturally ventilated structures. Pictured here are timber louvres on the façade of the Landau Public Library in Germany.

see Environmental Control 95, Cooling 62, Heating 122

L Lumsden at Small Back Room

Lumsden at Small Back Room, formerly known as Lumsden Design Partnership, is the retail design team within Small Back Room, which was set up by Callum Lumsden in 1994. The London-based multidisciplinary design firm specialises in interior design, architecture and graphic design. They have designed retail spaces in some of the most high-profile museums in Britain including the Tate Modern and the Victoria & Albert Museum (pictured below), as well as product design for museums and museum shops across the UK.

M Machine Aesthetic

THE HOUSE IS A MACHINE FOR LIVING IN

THE ADVENT OF INDUSTRIALISATION, MECHANISATION AND THE CONSTRUCTION OF THINGS BY MACHINES IN THE LATE NINETEENTH AND EARLY TWENTIETH CENTURIES, WHICH LED TO A NEW AESTHETIC BEING DEVELOPED. THE AESTHETIC OF OBJECTS AND ARTEFACTS PRODUCED BY MACHINES BEGAN TO BE REGARDED BY SOME DESIGNERS AND ARCHITECTS AS THE PINNACLE OF PERFECTION. THESE CREATORS BECAME KNOWN VARIOUSLY AS THE MODERNISTS, FUTURISTS, FUNCTIONALISTS AND CONSTRUCTIVISTS. THIS AESTHETIC DOMINATED ARCHITECTURE FOR MOST OF THE TWENTIETH CENTURY, A PERIOD KNOWN AS THE MODERN ERA.

☞ see Constructivism 60, Modernism 168–169

M Mackintosh, Charles Rennie 156

PERHAPS THE BEST KNOWN OF SCOTTISH ARCHITECTS AND DESIGNERS, CHARLES RENNIE MACKINTOSH (1886–1928) IS NOTED FOR THE GLASGOW SCHOOL OF ART. MACKINTOSH ESTABLISHED A STYLE THAT WAS UNIQUELY HIS, DRAWING ON HIS BEAUX-ARTS TRAINING AND THE MODERN INFLUENCE OF THE ARTS AND CRAFTS IN ENGLAND AND ART NOUVEAU IN FRANCE. PICTURED ABOVE IS THE INTERIOR OF HILL HOUSE IN HELENSBURGH, SCOTLAND.

see Art Nouveau 28, Arts and Crafts 29

M Magazines

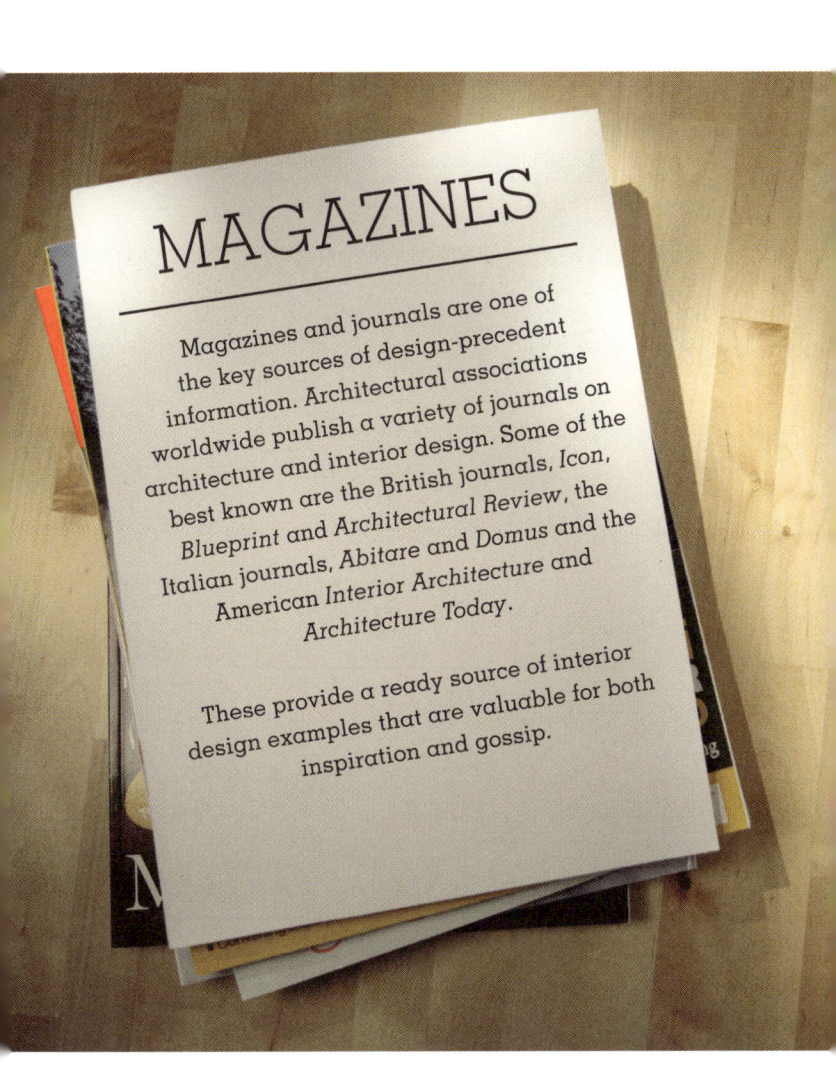

MAGAZINES

Magazines and journals are one of the key sources of design-precedent information. Architectural associations worldwide publish a variety of journals on architecture and interior design. Some of the best known are the British journals, Icon, Blueprint and Architectural Review, the Italian journals, Abitare and Domus and the American Interior Architecture and Architecture Today.

These provide a ready source of interior design examples that are valuable for both inspiration and gossip.

M Mannerism

A sixteenth-century architectural style characterised by distortions of scale and perspective and also symbolised by extreme sophistication and complexity. The style developed in Italy but spread to other European countries. Principal examples include the Uffizi in Florence by Vasari, Michelangelo's Medici Chapel and the Laurentian Library (pictured below).

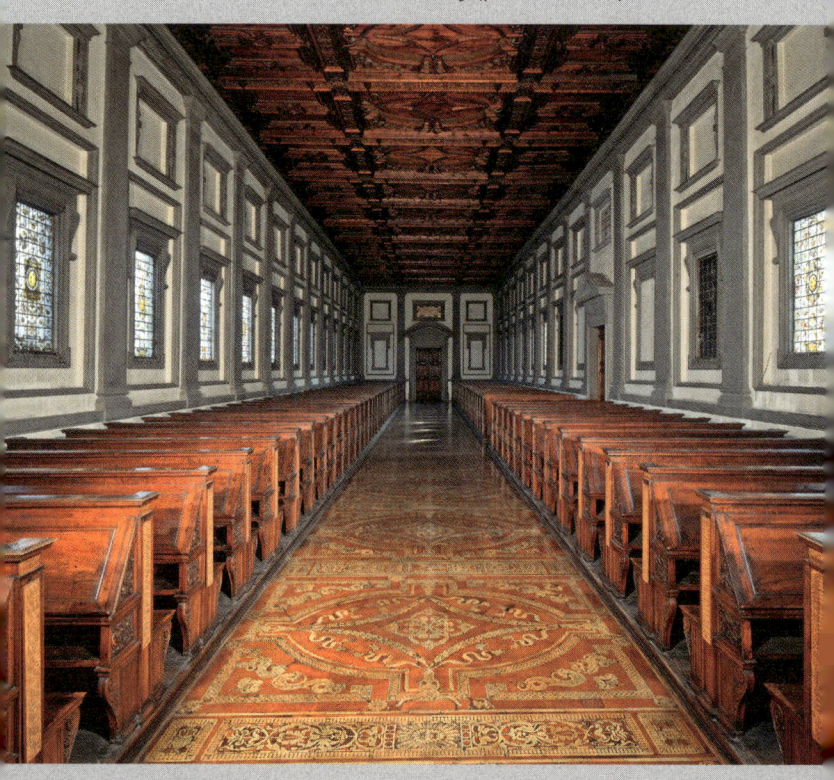

Mare, André

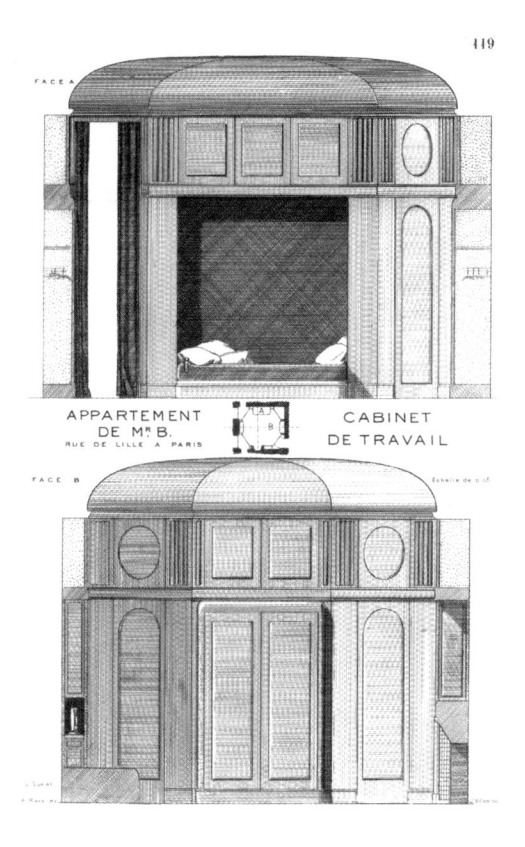

An artist who, in 1919 together with art deco interior designer, Louis Sue, established the practice Sue et Mare. Mare (1887–1932) involved himself with Raymond Duchamp-Villon, the brother of Marcel Duchamp. They designed the cubist house, the Maison Cubiste, in Paris (1912), which was unfortunately never built. The practice worked in all aspects of interior decoration; their furniture used exotic timber and was inspired by traditional French Louis Seize design. Illustrated here is Mare and Sue's Cabinet de Travail. The etching is by Marcel Duchamp's brother, Jacques Villon.

M Materials

Brick:
Still the primary building material used for homes and small-scale construction. Made from fired clay, the brick has been used in building since the Roman era.

Concrete:
Often thought of as a modern material, concrete was first used during the Roman era and, since the advent of modernism, it has been connected with contemporary buildings. It is another hugely versatile and incredibly hard-wearing material.

Glass:
A material that can be used to decorative effect as it ranges in opacity and comes in a variety of colours. Glass is now used frequently and lavishly throughout buildings, sometimes even structurally, such as its use in the modern skyscraper.

161

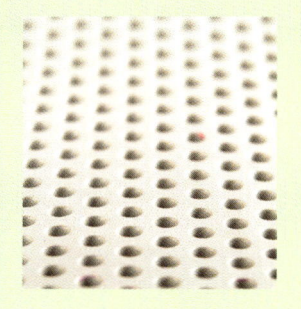

Plastic:
A derivative of oil, plastic is a versatile material used for many things, from the chips in computers to building façades. Plastics or polymers are easy to use, colour and shape, making them an immensely convenient material.

Stone:
A traditional material used for building from the very earliest days. It has been used historically to build all types of buildings, from homes to defensive walls. It can also be used more delicately or decoratively, or cut very thinly as a cladding material.

Timber:
A sustainable and readily available material, one of the first building materials that man made use of. Timber is used as the primary building material of homes in North America and Scandinavia.

M Matta Clark, Gordon 162

The American artist best known for his site-specific art in the 1970s, Matta Clark's (1943–1978) most famous work is the *Building Cuts* series (pictured below). With these projects he cut entire sections from derelict buildings, removing parts of the floors and walls and in some cases entire slices of the whole building, and displayed them in prestigious galleries and museums such as the Museum of Modern Art in New York. Matta Clark took the buildings and turned them into works of art in their own right, reinventing the way in which the observer sees them.

M Mezzanine

A half or intermediate floor of a building situated within a double-height space. The mezzanine was a common element in modernist architecture where the pursuit of light and space was a major driving force. It was used widely by Le Corbusier who was inspired by the Parisian art studios of his friends (usually one large space with a raised platform). He employed it widely in his domestic architecture, most famously in the double-height living rooms of the interlocking apartments of the Unité d'Habitation, Marseille.

The foyer of the National Museum of Scotland in Edinburgh, designed by Benson and Forsyth, makes use of a mezzanine floor.

☞ see Domestic 77, Le Corbusier 145

M Mies van der Rohe, Ludwig 164

A German-American architect (1886–1969) who was a pioneer of modern architecture. Through the use of modern construction materials such as steel and glass, he advanced the international style, which is characterised by simplicity and clarity. He encapsulated the style with aphorisms such as 'God is in the details' and 'less is more'. He was the director of architecture at the Bauhaus, where he advocated the use of simple geometric forms. His international style became the accepted model for buildings used for large corporations in America, where he lived from the late 1930s.

The pool at the rear of Mies van der Rohe's German National Pavilion for the 1929 Barcelona International Exhibition. The building was widely considered a modernist pièce de résistance.

see Chair 49, Le Corbusier 145, Modernism 168–169

M Minimalism

The minimalist aesthetic of the Novy Dvur monastery by John Pawson creates a simple and noble interior backdrop for contemplation in the Cistercian monk brotherhood.

A form of art, design and architecture that emerged in the West in the 1950s. The intention of minimalism was to create art that thrived on simplicity of form and content, removing any sign of personal expressiveness. It has become one of most populist forms of interior design and decoration. The use of sheer white surfaces (which root from modernism), planes of single materials and limited colour palettes have come to be perceived as the height of good taste.

see Modernism 168–169, Plane 189, Surface 238

Mirroring is a tactic used to organise space and form, most commonly seen in the symmetrical façades of classical buildings. Symmetrical façades are exact mirror images of each other when split along the central axis. This proportion was considered so 'right' as to be divine and is most prevalent in religious buildings. Mirroring is a device for organising space, where two sides of a space are symmetrical about an axis. Mirroring can also be used in the literal sense, through the application of a reflective surface.

The asymmetric folded planes of the outer wall of the Barcelona Forum by Herzog & de Meuron are exaggerated by the mirrored panels, which are set into the façade.

see Classical 52, Façade 99, Symmetry 240

M Model 167

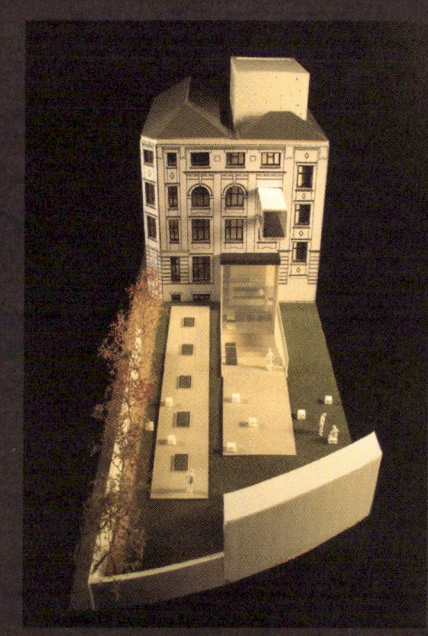

An architectural model is the best way of communicating the scale and 'feel' of a space. The sketch model (also known as a maquette) is usually quick to build and is made of paper or card. It can enable the designer to explain the interrelationship of spaces clearly.

A presentation model is a much more exquisite composition. Models are now more commonly associated with computer drawings. A computer can use two-dimensional drawings to construct a three-dimensional drawing or model of an interior. The cardboard and plastic model shown here was used to demonstrate a final-year student's design concept.

☛ see Scale 222

M Modernism

A movement in design, architecture and society that defined the modern world and flourished between 1890 and 1960. Modernism's golden age was in the inter-war period in Europe (1920–1939), when it produced some of the greatest architects and designers and consequently some of the most significant buildings and interiors. It was born out of a number of artistic movements of the late nineteenth and early twentieth centuries, including De Stijl from the Netherlands and the Bauhaus from Germany, both of which were responses to mechanisation and the change in the nature of production and design. European modernist architects such as Le Corbusier, Ludwig Mies van der Rohe, Walter Gropius and Berthold Lubetkin, to name a few, began to coalesce. The most tangible result of this coming together was the Congrés International d'Architecture Moderne (CIAM).

Modernists believed architecture played a major part in ensuring the well-being of society as a whole. Developing what became known as the machine aesthetic, they argued that a sufficient level of perfection could be achieved in architecture, particularly housing architecture, thus ensuring the ideal environment for human existence.

Facing page: The iconic bathroom in Le Corbusier's Villa Savoye demonstrates puritanical modernist design with the use of pure colours and sheer clean surfaces. The sunken bath tub is made of blue glass tiles and the chaise longue made of grey glass tiles. This is one of the most famous houses of the modernist movement and an example of Le Cobusier's machine for living ideal.

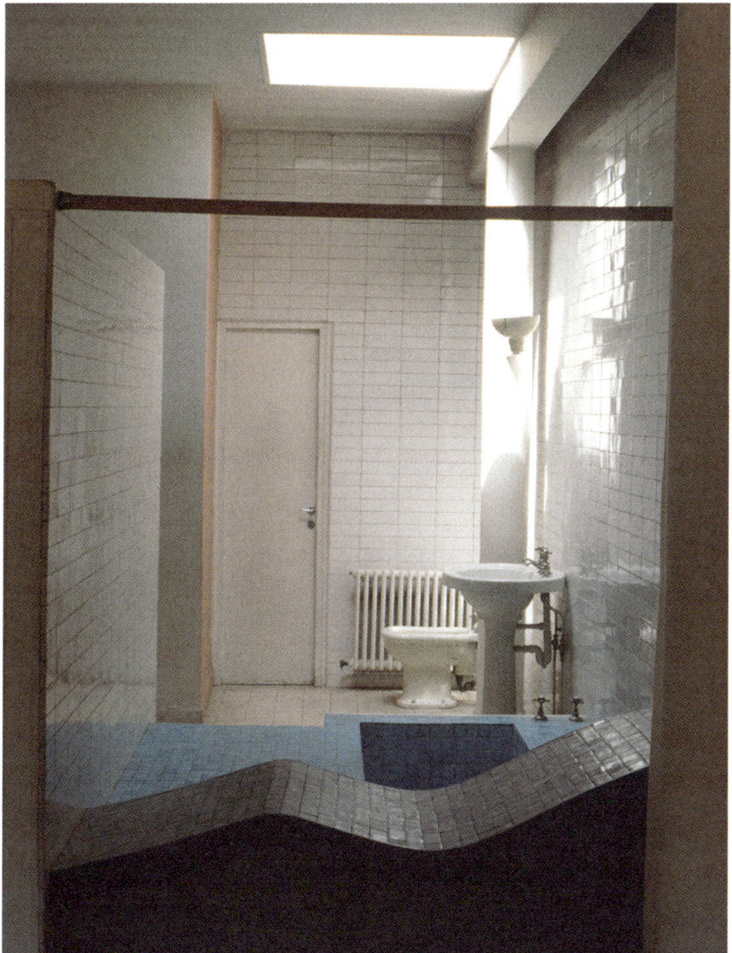

M Modular   170

The Murray Grove housing scheme in Bethnal Green, London, by Cartwright Pickard. It is an assemblage of modular Yorkon cabins, fitted out in factories and craned into place on site.

Of, relating to, or based upon modules or a module. In design it refers to an object designed with standardised units or dimensions for ease of assembly and flexibility of use. Modular furniture and modular buildings have been produced on a huge scale since the post-war period and the advent of mass production. The use of standardised elements has also enabled the prefabrication of dwellings and other items, in which the parts of an object are produced in a factory and then assembled on site. Modular must not be confused with Modulor, the system of proportion based upon the male figure, developed by Le Corbusier.

☞ see Element 88, Furniture 113

M Morris, William 171

An English artist and writer, Morris (1834–1896) was a pioneer of socialism in Britain and his ideas coincided with those of the Arts and Crafts Movement. He is best known as a writer and designer of wallpaper and textiles (such as his design for a bed canopy at his home at Kelmscott Manor, shown below). Morris, like many in the Arts and Crafts Movement, longed to preserve some sort of idealised pre-industrial England. To this end, in 1877 he started the Society for the Protection of Ancient Buildings (SPAB).

see Arts and Crafts 29, Ruskin, John 220

M Movement 172

In design, movement is concerned with the direction or path that a person takes through a space. Therefore a primary concern is 'directing' and 'facilitating' circulation and controlling it: speeding it up when necessary and slowing or even stopping it at times. It is therefore related to circulation areas, which provide spaces for movement. Movement is enabled by lifts, corridors and stairs, amongst others. It can also refer to styles or fashions in design. Modernism and De Stijl, for example, are referred to as design movements.

Pictured is the Tate Modern in London, where dynamic vertical circulation animates the interior space.

see Circulation 50, De Stijl 72, Modernism 168–169

N Narrative

From the Latin *narrare*, meaning 'to recount', a narrative is a story or series of events. A design may be considered to have a 'narrative context' relating to historic precepts in design and architecture. Narrative can also be used to refer to the arrangement of spaces in an interior and how the user is encouraged or directed through them. Exhibition design in particular employs this tactic to create a narrative of events. In order to develop narratives between the objects in the Castelvecchio Museum (pictured above), Carlo Scarpa deliberately positioned the sculptures and paintings in such a manner that they reveal the story of the place.

N Nash, John

John Nash was an English architect and planner of English romanticism, best known for his planning of Regent's Park, Park Crescent and Regent Street in London. Nash (1752–1835) came to the attention of the Prince Regent (later George IV) and was commissioned by him to remodel Brighton Pavilion (pictured here) between 1815–1822 and Buckingham Palace in 1825. Nash designed and built many other stately homes in Britain and was also responsible for the landscaping of their gardens. His name is synonymous with classical good taste.

Novembre, Fabio

An Italian architect, product designer and graphic artist credited for the great success of mosaic tile manufacturer Bisazza. The interior designs he produced for the company brought it global attention with showrooms in Milan, Berlin, New York and Barcelona. Novembre began studying film-making in New York but realised that cinematic concepts could be translated into three dimensions as interiors. He has courted controversy by turning up in magazine photo shoots dressed as icons such as Che Guevara and Jesus. He is pictured here with his S.O.S. chair.

O Object

A tangible or material thing in space that can be seen or touched. In design, an object is placed within a space to achieve a certain end. Elements such as furniture may be considered objects, but the term can be equally applied to things ranging up in size to entire sections of buildings or new insertions. Spaces such as museums and art galleries are designed around the objects to be exhibited. This makes the space in these environments subservient to the objects.

This bust is a free-standing object that is strategically placed in the main exhibition hall of the National Museum of Roman Art, Merida, Spain.

☛ see Element 88, Space 233

O Offices 177

Office space is a very particular form of interior design. The majority of office spaces are built as large open-plan spaces for maximum flexibility. However, the concept of the 'new office', which was popularised by Frank Duffy of DEGW Architects, is becoming more prevalent. This is the idea that office users occupy a space most suitable for the task they perform, rather than permanently sitting in the same place. He catalogued the different types of spaces that office workers needed and these are classified as the hive, the cell, the den and the club. Pictured above is a semi-private meeting room in the office scheme for XAP Corporation in Culver City, California, designed by Pugh-Scarpa.

O Openings   178

The term 'opening' is used to describe any aperture in a surface, be it a wall, floor or ceiling. Conventionally, an opening will either be filled with a window or used to allow circulation, such as doorways or stairwells. However, openings can occasionally be employed to provide a view or accentuate some aspect of a scheme to which the designer wants to draw the viewer's attention. In the photograph above, this method has been utilised by designers EMBT in their design of Utrecht Town Hall. The view from the exterior to the interior of the building is framed by large apertures.

☞ see Circulation 50, Window 263

O Ornament

Ornament is the embellishment of an object or building with decorative and possibly purposeless design work. A picture frame may be heavily ornamented; it can be carved and gilded in a bid to communicate wealth and luxury. These additions do not improve the functionality and in some cases are used actively to hide bad craftsmanship and have merely an aesthetic purpose. In interior architecture and design, ornament is less an object and more an act or – in the opinion of Adolf Loos, a forerunner of the modernist movement – 'a crime'.

Pictured is the embellished and heavily ornamented ceiling and light fixtures of the Brighton Pavilion, UK, designed by John Nash in 1815–1823.

see Loos, Adolf 151, Modernism 168–169, Nash, John 174

P Painting

180

The act of painting a space is used in all interior design and decoration. It has both a practical and aesthetic purpose. A coat of paint protects the surface of walls against dirt and damp while allowing the use of flat colour to decorate a space. Paints with different properties will be used in different rooms depending on their function. Waterproof paint is used in bathrooms and kitchens, water-based emulsion is generally used internally, while gloss, which is oil-based and therefore much more hard and resilient, is used for painting wood and exterior work.

Illustrated is the interior of Oslo City Hall. Its walls are painted with symbolic images of important moments in Norway's history.

☛ see Interior Decoration 131

P Palladio, Andrea

Andrea Palladio (1508-1580) is considered to be one of the most influential figures in the history of Western architecture. He adhered to the principles of classical architecture, most notably the Roman symmetrical planning and harmonic proportions. David Watkin wrote in *A History of Western Architecture*, 'Palladio has been valued for centuries as the quintessence of high Renaissance calm and harmony'. Palladio came to broad attention with his *Quattro Libri dell'Architettura* (The Four Books of Architecture) in 1570.

The perfectly symmetrical Villa Rotunda in Vicenza, Italy, is organised around the central rotunda, which is top lit and decorated with extravagant paintings.

See Classical 52

P Partition

Pictured is the screen wall partition in the Charnley House in Chicago. The partition separates the staircase from the landing and allows natural light into the interior below.

Principally an element used to divide a space and enable it to perform a specific function. Partitions can be permanent, such as plasterboard wall partitions used in interiors. They are not load-bearing structures but they create rooms and can be removed without affecting the structural integrity of the building. Temporary, portable and sliding partitions are used to divide up larger open-plan spaces.

☛ see Load Bearing 150, Wall 259

P Pattern

A decorative and usually repeating design such as chevrons or Paisley. Employed in interior decoration on furniture, wallpapers and curtains for hundreds of years, floral patterns are particularly common. They are used as a form of decoration in Islamic art and the interiors of mosques, such as the one pictured below, are decorated with geometric patterns as imagery is forbidden. Patterns applied to concrete, glass and other more architectural surfaces have become increasingly popular at the beginning of the twenty-first century.

see Geometry 115, Textile Design 243

P Perriand, Charlotte 184

French architect, designer and collaborator of Le Corbusier, Perriand (1903-1999) first came to the design world's attention in 1927, when she exhibited at the Salon d'Automne Paris. Her steel and aluminium bar furniture attracted a great deal of attention and not only from Le Corbusier. She went on to design the interiors, fixtures and fittings on some of Le Corbusier's most notable projects. In 1998, the year before she died, she was honoured with a hugely popular retrospective at the Design Museum in London.

The iconic tubular steel and leather chaise longue was designed by Perriand and Le Corbusier to relax the user and to help stimulate the blood flow in the sitter's raised legs.

see Le Corbusier 145

P Perspective

This one-point perspective portrays a dynamic and direct view of the space in this student proposal for a chapel.

Perspective describes the appearance of objects at a distance, as well as the effect of distance on the perception of objects. Perspective is also a form of representation, in that perspective drawing is a tool used to create three-dimensional views of spaces on a two-dimensional surface. The drawing can be a one-, two-, or three-point perspective, depending on the sort of view that is required.

☞ see Drawing 81

P Piano Nobile

The principal floor of a house and the most important within the spatial hierarchy. This floor usually contains the main reception or public rooms and is often on the first floor in older Renaissance or classical period houses. As a result the rooms would have finer views and are raised from the noise and grime of the street, but more practically avoid damp. This is particularly evident in the large houses of Venice where the piano nobile floor is indicated by the larger and more ornate windows.

The first floor of the Villa Rotunda in Vicenza, pictured, exemplifies the piano nobile as it contains the important rooms, such as the reception and entertaining spaces of the house.

P Piloti 187

Illustrated is the Villa Savoye in Poissy, France, by Le Corbusier. The building is raised up on the piloti in order to allow the landscape to flow underneath the building.

Piloti

One of the elements identified by Le Corbusier in his famous five points of architecture. Piloti are essentially structural columns that support all the weight of the structure and release the plan and the façade from structural constraints. Le Corbusier uses piloti extensively in his villas and in some of his larger scale housing projects to allow the landscape to flow ostensibly beneath the buildings. It is an architectural form that has been repeated by modern and contemporary architects all over the world.

☞ see Column 57, Le Corbusier 145

P Plan 188

A plan is a two-dimensional drawing or diagram of the floor layout of a space. Conventionally a plan is the space viewed from above, providing a bird's-eye view without perspective. The vertical elements such as walls and fixed furniture are conventionally cut a metre above the floor itself, thus allowing the positions of the windows to be indicated. Along with the section and the model, it is the most useful tool a designer can employ when organising a space.

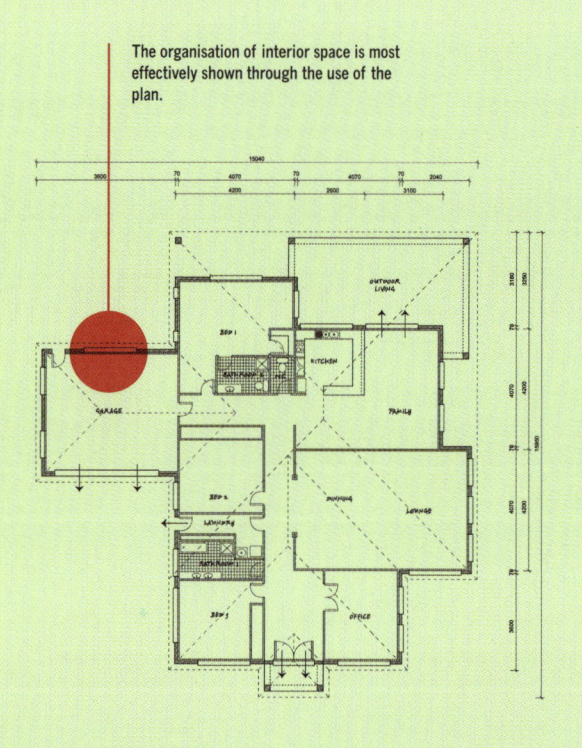

The organisation of interior space is most effectively shown through the use of the plan.

see Drawing 81, Model 167

P Plane 189

In design terminology, a plane is a flat surface of any sort, such as a floor, wall or ceiling. These planes define and control the space. In the Schröder House by Gerrit Rietveld, the walls slide past each other, forming an assemblage of planes that appear to hang in space. In the Barcelona Pavilion by Mies van der Rohe, the vertical wall planes create a view into and through the pavilion, while the horizontal roof and floor planes extend out and beyond the edge of the building.

The wall of the Basis Wien links the interior and exterior and advertises the function of the space to the visitor to the Museum Quarter in Vienna.

see Mies van der Rohe, Ludwig 164

P Ponti, Giò

An Italian architect, furniture and product designer, Giò Ponti (1891–1979) is famous for the Pirelli Tower, Milan's first skyscraper. He also worked in ceramics, producing items of sanitaryware for Ideal Standard and Richard Ginori. He worked for the Italian furniture company Cassina, where he was responsible for Superleggera (Super-light), a chair light enough to be lifted by a child using just one finger. He is also remembered for founding the arts and design magazine *Domus*, a journal that is still well respected today.

Illustrated is the classic Superleggera Chair designed for Cassina by Giò Ponti in 1957.

see Magazines 157

P Portico

A magnificent colonnaded portico announces the entrance to the US Supreme Court building, conveying the power and gravity of the American legal system.

A porch or colonnade-type structure usually fronting a classical building. A portico traditionally consists of a series of columns or a colonnade supporting a pediment, which often represents the building's purpose. The portico first emerged in Greco-Roman temples and public buildings. Its chief function was to signal the entrance and provide shading over it, which helped to reduce the interior temperature.

☛ see Classical 52, Column 57, Frieze 111

P Post and Beam

A collection of structural elements consisting of vertical uprights or posts supporting a horizontal beam. This method of construction is often described as post and lintel or trabeated, and is commonly found in ancient Greek architecture. Post-and-beam structures are restricted in the amount of weight they can support and the length of the beam limits the distance between the two support posts. These limitations led the Romans to develop the arch.

The column and the beam, pictured, at the ruined Temple of Poseidon, Greece, constitute the basic structural elements of architecture.

see Arch 22, Structure 237

P Postmodernism

The antithesis of and reaction to modernism, postmodernism rejects high-modernist culture in architecture, art and society in general and it attempts to reimpose a sense of historicism on design. It uses a process of making reference to old forms and precepts and mimicking building styles and techniques. Emerging as a movement in the 1960s–1970s, postmodernism initially tried to make design easy to grasp by creating deliberate references to recognisable forms that contained inherent meaning. Twenty-first century postmodern theory connects many areas associated with contemporary consumer culture, hyper-reality and anaesthetic architecture, which results in an inevitable incoherence. It has been described as the architecture of Western capitalism, with particular reference to architecture in New York and Chicago.

The postmodernist Piazza d' Italia by Charles Moore in New Orleans, USA, relies on mimicry to give meaning through powerful associations with the past.

see Coates, Nigel 54, Hyper-Reality 127

P Prefabricated 194

This term refers to buildings or building elements that are manufactured off site in a factory and then transported to the site to be erected. It is common practice for timber houses in North America to be prefabricated in panels and then put together on site. This results in a quicker process with less disruption, noise, waste and danger, which are inherent in the building process. Prefabricated (or prefab) buildings can also be built as modules that are combined to create temporary buildings for schools or, in the case of the immediate post-war period, emergency housing.

The Morton Loft in New York by LOT-EK was constructed by installing a prefabricated container in the space, to create two sleeping pods raised above the main living area.

☛ see Modular 170, LOT-EK 152

P Presentation

A presentation is a vital part of design and is the act of communicating ideas to others. The designer will present to a client and to a planning committee while those in education use the method to present to their peers and tutors. A verbal presentation will always be accompanied by a series of drawings, visuals and models, as illustrated above, that communicate the most important aspect of the design. It is a vital tool in design education, enabling the tutor and the student to communicate directly over the nature of the scheme and for the students to demonstrate their design ideas.

☛ see Model 167, Perspective 185, Plan 188, Scheme 224

P Private/Public 196

Spaces within an interior can be defined as private or public. Certain areas in a building are designated for general use and are therefore public areas, while other spaces are much more specific and limited and would therefore be private areas. The interior of Farnsworth House by Mies van der Rohe (pictured below) is opened to the exterior using expanses of glass. This transparent wall blurs the boundary between public and private space.

☞ see Building 42

P Product Design

The iconic Juicy Salif, by Philippe Starck for Alessi, is a classic example of product design.

The discipline that concerns itself with the design of three-dimensional objects and commodities, as opposed to spatial, interior, graphic or textile design. Largely associated with domestic and consumer durables, it can extend to furniture, cars or even larger objects. Product design is not beyond many designers who are principally thought of as architects. Le Corbusier, Frank Lloyd Wright, Charles Rennie Mackintosh and Ludwig Mies van der Rohe have all designed objects of varying scale in a building, from the ink pots for the bureau to the fitted kitchens and other furniture.

☞ see Gesamtkunstwerk 116, Le Corbusier 145, Starck, Philippe 236

P Proportion

The relationship between the parts or the dimensions of an element. For example, the ancient Greeks considered the ratio of the sides of a room or even that of the whole house to be harmonious if the lengths of the sides were in the ratio of 1:2, 2:3 or 2:4. The golden rectangle is an irrational proportion, which is considered by the Renaissance theorists to be divine. It has the ratio of approximately 5:8.

0, 1, 1, 2, 3, 5, 8, 13, 21, 34, 55, 89, 144, 233, 377, 610, 987, 1597, 2584, 4181, 6765, 10946, 17711, 28657...

Fibonacci's discovery of a series of numbers where each number is the sum of the preceding two has become a cornerstone of design practice. Their link to the 5:8 ratio (as the series progresses, the ratio of a Fibonacci number to its predecessor gets closer to 1.618: the Golden Section) means that they are believed by many to provide the basis of a balanced and well proportioned design.

☛ see Golden Section 117, Object 176, Scale 222

P Psychology   199

The arrangement and colour of the fantasy landscape interiors pictured, were designed by Verner Panton in order to impact upon the mood and disposition of the occupier of the space.

The science of the mind. The psychology of space affects many forms of design and the manner in which a space can impact upon a person psychologically can depend on a number of factors, including the level of light, the position of the windows, the arrangement of the furniture and the colour of the walls. It is a subject of interest to many architects and designers especially Steven Holl and Joseph Rykwert. The phenomenology of architecture is a related discipline that explores how and why meaning is assigned to places. Psychology of space can also be employed in retail design in order to create environments which are conducive to the purchase of goods.

see Holl, Steven 126, Retail Design 213, Space 233

Q Quadrangle

200

A QUADRANGLE OR 'QUAD' IS A FORM OF ARCHITECTURAL COMPOSITION DERIVED FROM THE ECCLESIASTICAL DESIGN OF THE CLOISTER. IT IS COMMONLY EMPLOYED IN PUBLIC AND EDUCATIONAL BUILDINGS. IT IS AN OPEN COURTYARD, WHICH IS ENCLOSED WITHIN THE BUILDING. THE QUAD IS PROBABLY BEST KNOWN AS A FEATURE OF THE COLLEGES OF OXFORD AND CAMBRIDGE, ENGLAND. IT IS IN EFFECT AN OUTSIDE ROOM, A NEGATIVE SPACE OR VOID, CREATED BY THE ARRANGEMENT OF POSITIVE OR SOLID SPACES.

The quadrangle of All Souls, Cambridge, as seen from above, is open to the elements and is surrounded by richly decorated façades.

Qualification

A higher educational qualification such as a degree can be gained in the field of interior design and in the UK it is classified as a Bachelor of Arts; most universities offer programmes in the study of interiors. A degree in interior architecture, interior design and interior decoration enables the graduate to undertake a career in design. Unfortunately, there is still not a recognised and regulated profession for interior designers, unlike architects, who have a protected and regulated professional title.

Q Quatrefoil

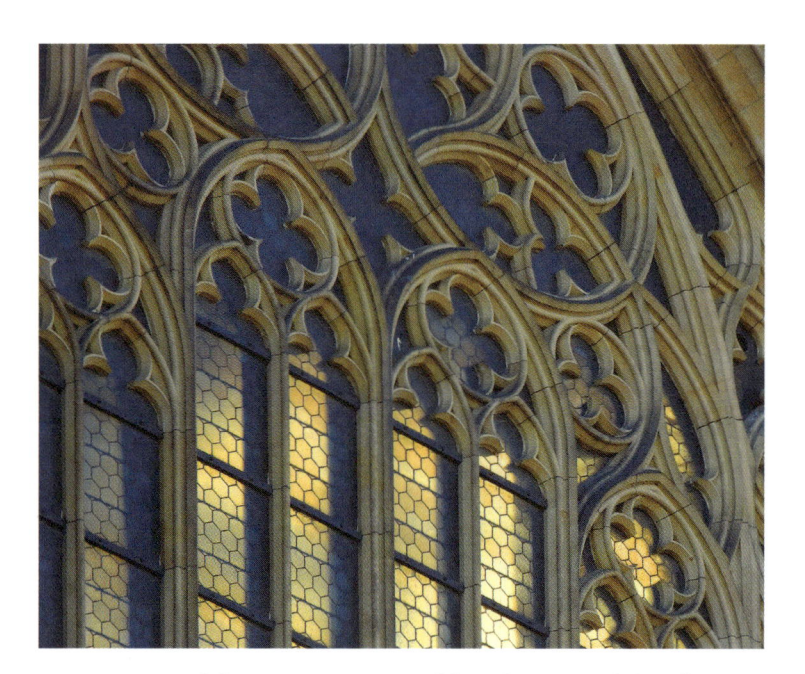

An ornamental design consisting of four leaves or lobes formed by the cusping of a circle or an arch. Quatrefoil, French for 'four leaf', is the most commonly used of the foil forms, the others being trefoil (three leaves), sexfoil (six leaves) and multifoil (many leaves). These are most commonly found in Gothic buildings, such as St Vitus Cathedral in Prague, Czech Republic (shown here).

☞ see Window 263

Q Quoin

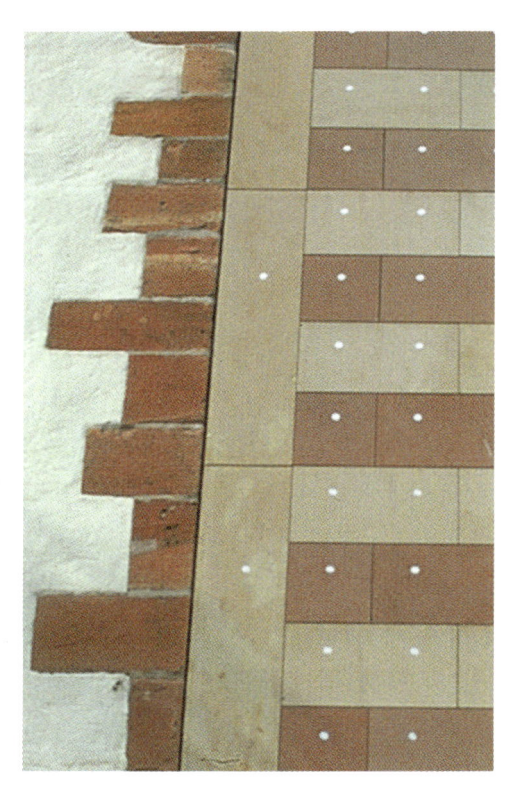

Where new meets old at the Museum of PreHistory, Frankfurt: the designer Josef Kleihues placed the new stone-clad building (right) against the quoins of the old (left).

A quoin is the dressed stone at the corner of a building and as such it is similar to a wedge or cornerstone. They are usually laid alternately to help project elevation and provide rubble or less strong walls with strength and rigidity. The surfaces of the quoin may be significantly different, such as the cut-stone quoins on a rendered building.

☛ see Edge 86, Structure 237, Surface 238

R Ranalli, George

Ranalli is a practising architect and designer based in New York, USA. His portfolio includes urban design and landscaping as well as new-build domestic architecture, renovations and restorations of landmark buildings. He is internationally known for his work in historic settings and he designs buildings and additions, which, although new, seem to blend seamlessly into the urban context. His projects, such as the interior living space of the K-Loft apartment in New York (shown below), clearly demonstrate his roots in the craft tradition of design and architecture.

R Randy Brown Architects 205

The architect's own studio and residence in Omaha, USA reflects the aesthetic concerns of the practice. Pictured is the meeting room.

A practice that began modestly as Randy Brown Interiors in the 1980s but rapidly expanded into a multidisciplinary design firm concerned with the actual construction of buildings, as well as the design of the interiors. Brown works primarily in his home city of Omaha, Nebraska, where he takes inspiration from the area's rural life. The vernacular forms of agricultural buildings permeate his design proposals, as do the materials of wooden and corrugated metal outbuildings. He was educated at the University of California, Los Angeles, and was taught and influenced by high-profile architects such as Daniel Libeskind and Frank Gehry.

R Raumplan

A three-dimensional planning and organisational device developed by the Viennese architect Adolf Loos. It is best exemplified in the designs for the Müller House in Prague and Moller House in Vienna. These houses consist of a series of compact, enclosed and intimately connected rooms. The spaces have an internal focus and the movement between them is often organised in a circular manner. Views generally extend through a series of internal spaces, rather than connecting with the outside. The exteriors of the buildings are surprisingly balanced and possibly even severe, given the richness of the interior organisation.

'My architecture is not conceived by drawings, but by spaces. I do not draw plans, facades or sections... For me, the ground floor, first floor do not exist... There are only interconnected continual spaces, rooms, halls, terraces... Each space needs a different height... These spaces are connected so that ascent and descent are not only unnoticeable, but at the same time functional.'

Adolf Loos

☛ see Loos, Adolf 151, Modernism 168–169

R Reflection

Reflection is the literal mirror image of an object on a surface and also the more conceptual idea of balancing elements within a design. Pictured is the interior of Sir John Soane's Museum in London, which is distorted by a series of strategically placed mirrors.

see Façade 99, Mirror 166, Symmetry 240

R Regency

Regency refers to the period of British history during the rule of the Prince Regent (1811–1820), (later to become King George IV). The fashion closely followed the neo-classical Georgian style of architecture (1720–1840), with added elegance and lightness of touch. The key practitioner of English Regency architecture was Sir John Nash, who is famed for his magnificent terraces on Regent Street and Regent's Park (pictured here) in London.

☞ see Nash, John 174

R Reichen et Robert

Philippe Robert and Bernard Reichen established the practice of Reichen et Robert in 1973. They have a reputation for their focus on conversion projects and their sensitive approach to the reuse and redesign of existing buildings. This contextual approach to dealing with existing buildings extends to the site and urban environment. They received international attention in 1987 for their reuse of the weaving mills of northern France and the publication of Robert's then rather radical book, *Adaptations*, in 1989.

Pictured are some of the interior elements of the redesigned former convent, Les Récollets, Paris, by Reichen et Robert, showing the interrelationship between the existing and the new.

see Reuse 214

R Remodelling

Remodelling, adaptive reuse or interior architecture all describe the process of making major alterations to a building in order to prepare it for a new use. This functional change is the most obvious modification, but other alterations may be made to the building and the spaces within it, such as its structure, circulation routes and orientation. This process may be radical, involving whole-scale demolition and reconstruction of all or certain aspects of the existing building. Pictured is the bookshop designed by Merkx + Girod architects who remodelled a former church in Maastricht, Holland, in order to install the Selexyz Dominicanen bookstore. While preserving the structure, a new use for the space was found.

☛ see Reuse 214

R Renaissance

Today the term 'Renaissance' means Italian art and architecture, which from 1420 until the middle of the sixteenth century was founded upon the restoration of the ancient Roman standards and motifs. It has its basis in the sense of stability and poise found in classical art.

The Renaissance, which is the French for 'rebirth', revolutionised attitudes towards philosophy, literature, politics, science, art and architecture.

Brunelleschi's works in Florence, Italy are considered by many to mark the beginning of the Renaissance, which gradually spread northwards throughout Europe.

☛ see Classical 52

R Restoration

212

Restoration is the process of returning the condition of a building to its original state. This often involves using materials and techniques of the original period to ensure that the building appears as though it has just been constructed. Sometimes long-dead and outdated techniques have to be revived and authentic materials sourced.

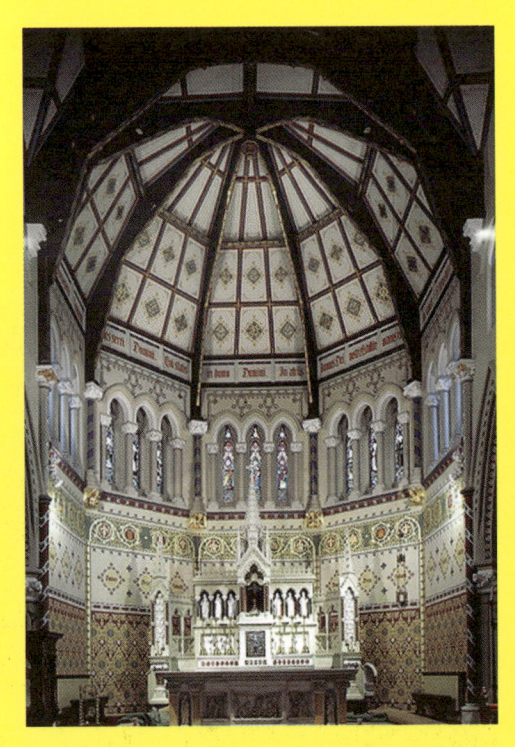

St Mary's Church of Barrow-in-Furness, UK was carefully restored before being painted in an appropriate traditional manner. This sensitive restoration of the E.W. Pugin building is by Francis Roberts Architects.

☛ see Conservation 59, Gothic Revival 118

R Retail Design 213

Retail design is an area in which interior architecture, design and decoration play an important role. The quality and character of the interior of a shop is absolutely vital to the space's commercial success. Different shops are designed in particular ways to reflect the specific concept the retailer wants to promote; the ideas that attract the sort of clientele they target to buy their products. Retail design is rooted in the psychology of shopping and the methods by which people are encouraged to spend money. Illustrated is the Choice store, designed by RAWFISH design consultants.

see Conservation 59, Space 233

R Reuse 214

Building reuse, adaptive reuse, remodelling and interior architecture are all terms that describe the process of reusing an existing building for a function that is different from its original purpose. This practice is central to the profession of interior design. The reuse of existing buildings and the redesign of spaces are important for the evolution of the urban environment and at the beginning of the twenty-first century, issues of conservation and sustainability have increasingly become vital to the development of cities. Interior design is at the very heart of this revolution.

New uses such as a gallery and gymnasium are contained within the timber-clad element inserted above the nave of St Paul's, Bow, London.

see Conservation 59, Remodelling 210, Sustainability 239

R Rococo

Not a style in its own right but the last phase of the baroque movement, rococo was prominent in early eighteenth-century France (1725–1775). It developed from baroque but was more playful and graceful; its decoration was light-hearted, aristocratic and carefree, with a focus on asymmetry, curves and natural forms, such as tree branches, clouds, flowers, seashells and spray. Detailing was frequently picked out in gold. Rooms were typically rectangular with rounded corners and flat, smooth walls that could be decorated. Woodwork around doors was often carved and the use of mirrors was common. The title is a derivative of the French *rocaille* meaning 'rockwork'. Rococo became popular with Louis XV's ascendancy to the French throne and the return of the monarch to the Palace of Versailles. Pictured is the extravagent interior of the Vierzehnheiligen Wallfahrtskirche, Germany.

☛ see Baroque 35

R Roman

The art, architecture and culture associated with the Ancient Roman Empire, which lasted from the ninth century BC to the fifth century AD across Europe. Roman architecture is essentially based upon the round arch and the dome; it moved away from the more primitive system of the post and lintel to develop a method of ordered construction that allowed huge fluid buildings to be constructed. The wall became more prominent, thus the enclosed space or room became a valued space. It can be argued that it was the Romans who marked the beginning of interior design. Another major development was the invention of concrete, which made it possible to construct huge domes such as that found in the Pantheon (pictured); the interior is a beautiful, enclosed top-lit room of massive proportions.

see Arch 22, Classical 52, Dome 76

R Room

Any separate and distinguishable space usually found within a building. It is separated from other spaces, rooms or corridors by interior walls or partitions. The room has evolved from a multi-functional space in which many and sometimes all activities occurred, to a specifically designed enclosed place for a single particular activity. The circular room at the centre of the Altes Museum in Berlin, Germany (pictured), was once referred to as the greatest room in the city.

☛ see Corridor 64, Partition 182, Space 233

R Rotunda

A circular building, or part of a building, may be described as a rotunda. This structure is usually, though not always, covered with a dome. The rotunda is a feature of many different styles of architecture, but it is most prevalent within the classical style.

The interior of the rotunda of the Texan Capitol Building, Dallas, USA.

see Classical 52, Dome 76

R Rural Studio

An American 'design and build' practice with a conscience, founded in 1993 by the late Sam Mockbee, whose own upbringing in segregated Mississippi gave him great awareness of the injustices of life in southern USA. Rural Studio builds unique homes and community buildings such as that illustrated for poor communities in western Alabama. These homes are constructed from reused and recycled materials to create cheap, yet well-designed and well-constructed houses.

R Ruskin, John

Pictured is a sketch by Ruskin of his beloved Venice.

An English architect, art critic, poet and social commentator. Ruskin (1819–1900) was one of the inspirations for the Arts and Crafts Movement, which attempted to move away from Victorian industrialisation and revert to a much more craft-based mode of production. These ideas are explored in his famous text of 1849, *The Seven Lamps of Architecture*. Ruskin was profoundly in favour of the Gothic style; he considered it to be a morally superior form of architecture, as opposed to classicism, which he associated with the evils of industrialisation.

see Arts and Crafts 29, Classical 52, Morris, William 171

S Sample

A small section or selection of materials chosen to show the designer or client what the whole is like. The designer generally obtains samples or swatches direct from the manufacturer. The composition of a sample board can show a number of different options of the same product, such as tiles or fabrics, or it can attempt to portray an essence of the whole project with an artfully arranged selection of all the different finishes.

see Materials 160–161

S Scale

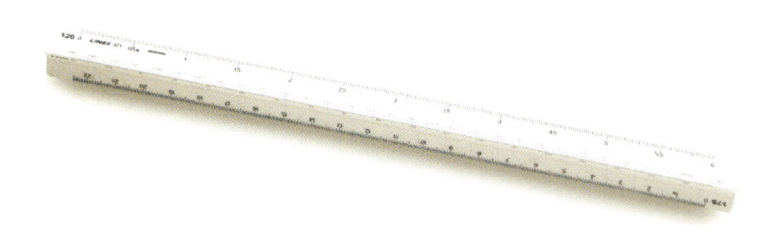

222

The size of objects in a scale drawing can be easily determined using a scale ruler. A scale ruler is a measuring instrument with a number of scale ratios 1:50, 1:100, 1:200, and so on marked out along its length.

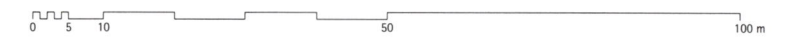

A scale ratio of size is used to provide the interior architect and designer information about the real-life size of elements represented in drawings and plans.

A measuring system based on the size of an element or object in relation to other objects or elements. The relationship of one thing to another determines how both are perceived. Scale also refers to a ratio of size in a map, model, drawing or plan. For example, a floor plan drawn at 1:100 scale is 100 times smaller than the actual space. Certain scales are generally used to communicate different aspects of a design proposal: 1:1000, 1:500 or larger are used for urban planning drawings; 1:200, 1:100, 1:50 are used for the general arrangement of spaces and 1:20, 1:10, 1:5, 1:2, 1:1 or even 2:1 are used for communicating details.

☞ see Drawing 81

Scarpa, Carlo

The Venetian architect and designer Carlo Scarpa (1906–1978) is noted for his profound understanding of the relevance of landscape and materiality within design, as well as his grasp of his native Venetian culture. Many of Scarpa's buildings are in Venice, which has a propensity to flood, and so the movement of the water is exploited and incorporated into many of his designs. An enduring feature of Scarpa's work was the inventive manner in which he handled the relationship of the old and new, the monumental and the everyday. One of Scarpa's best known projects is the Castelvecchio Museum in Verona, Italy, pictured below.

S Scheme

A plan or programme, a scheme is a way of approaching a problem. In design it is a broad term that refers to a proposal for a space. It is the name given to the new elements, or the plan for the design of a space or building. The manner in which the project interacts with the existing building is one of the most important factors within interior architecture and design. Models and drawings such as the one above can assist the designer in their approach to a problem and formulation of a scheme.

S Section

A TYPE OF REPRESENTATIONAL DRAWING OR DIAGRAM. AT ANY POINT ON THE PLAN OF A BUILDING, THE DESIGNER MAY DESCRIBE A LINE THROUGH THE DRAWING AND VISUALISE A VERTICAL CUT THROUGH THE SPACES. THIS IS CALLED A SECTION; IT WILL ILLUSTRATE THE VOLUME OF THE SPACES AND INDICATE THE POSITION OF THE WALLS, FLOORS, ROOF AND OTHER STRUCTURAL ELEMENTS. IT CONTAINS NO PERSPECTIVE AND IS USUALLY DRAWN AT AN EXACT SCALE, SUCH AS 1:100, 1:50 OR 1:20, DEPENDING UPON THE AMOUNT OF DETAIL REQUIRED.

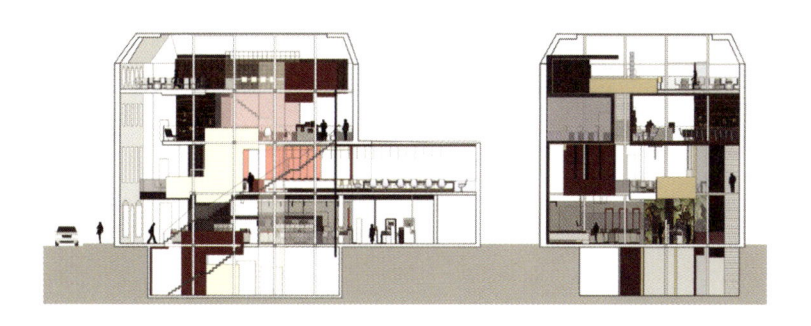

This sectional drawing of a student scheme shows the complex three-dimensional relationships that exist within a remodelled building.

see Drawing 81, Plan 188

Semper, Gottfried

One of the most important German architects of the nineteenth century, Gottfried Semper (1803–1879) believed that the function of a building should be shown within its plan and façade. Thus, the way a building looks should be an expression of its use. This included the exterior elevations and decorations on a building.

The Opera House in Dresden, Germany, is a fine example of the work of Semper. The functions of the interior are clearly articulated on the relaxed baroque exterior.

S Sequence 227

The arrangement or order in which spaces or elements are arranged. Sequence is related to architectural promenade and is a modernist method of creating movement within the interior of a building. The series of spaces within the Villa Rotunda (pictured above) create an enfilade or procession of rooms sequenced as a journey from the central rotunda to the landscape outside.

see Architectural Promenade 24, Scheme 224

S Served/Servant Space

The served areas of a building are at the top of the hierarchy of space, while the servant areas are at the bottom. Served spaces are those that are provided with services, therefore a restaurant's dining area is the served space and the kitchen is the servant space. However, the servant spaces may not necessarily be those that are traditionally occupied by the servants; for example, a parliamentary debating chamber is a served space – in this context it is served by offices, washrooms, bars and libraries. In the Restaurant Georges in the Pompidou Centre in Paris (pictured), some of the pods contain the kitchen, cloakroom and toilets while others house the exclusive eating and drinking spaces.

S Skirting

The strip of material horizontally placed along the point at which the interior wall meets the floor. It is usually made from painted wood but is also commonly constructed from metal, tile, plastic or stone. It is often made from the same material as the floor surface. Skirting is primarily used to hide the junction between two surfaces. Like the architrave and coving, it can be a decorative aspect of the interior, painted and embellished to enhance its presentation.

☛ see Architrave 26, Coving 66

S Soffit

230

A technical design term for what is conventionally known as the ceiling. The term soffit is also used to describe the underside of any element of a building, whether inside or outside, such as the underside of a staircase, balcony or arch.

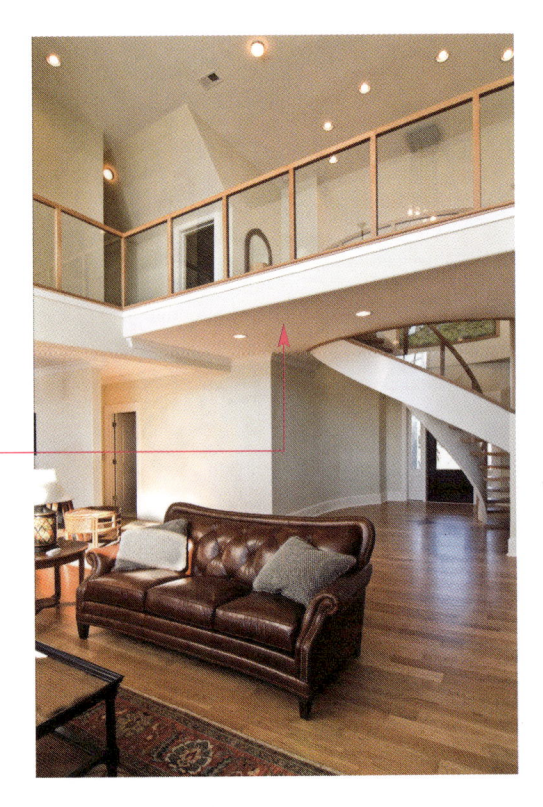

Soffit
The underside of the balcony, stairs and ceiling are all described as the soffit.

see Ceiling 48, Element 88, Plane 189

S Softroom

A UK-based multidisciplinary architectural practice that has gained a reputation for inventive and progressive design. Softroom have created designs for the BBC as well as having worked on interiors, architecture, exhibitions and transport design. Softroom have been praised by RIBA for their innovative and integrated sustainable designs and for their careful approach to working within existing buildings, landscapes and historical contexts. Pictured above is Softroom's design for the Virgin Atlantic Clubhouse at Heathrow Airport.

S Sottsass, Ettore 232

The eccentric Italian designer who founded the Milan-based Memphis collective in the 1980s. Sottsass (1917–2007) had previously worked for Olivetti, the electronic company, where in 1969 he designed the iconic bright red portable typewriter. However, it wasn't until he produced his famed *Carlton Cabinet* for the radical collective in 1981 that Sottsass really came to international attention.

S Space 233

The Turbine Hall in Tate Modern, London, is a large, high, interior space with cathedral-like proportions.

A generic term used to describe any interior or exterior environment or an enclosed area that is different from 'place', which is a specific space with identifiable characteristics. A room in a building can be described as a space; an outside area such as a courtyard or garden can be described as an exterior space. The nature and the feel of a space is vital to the success of a building.

see Room 217

S Stack Effect 234

The process of warm air rising though a space or building and being replaced with cooler air at a low level. As the hot air rises, it creates a temporary vacuum into which cooler, heavier air is pulled, thus creating a cooling breeze. This natural process can be used to cool a space or building.

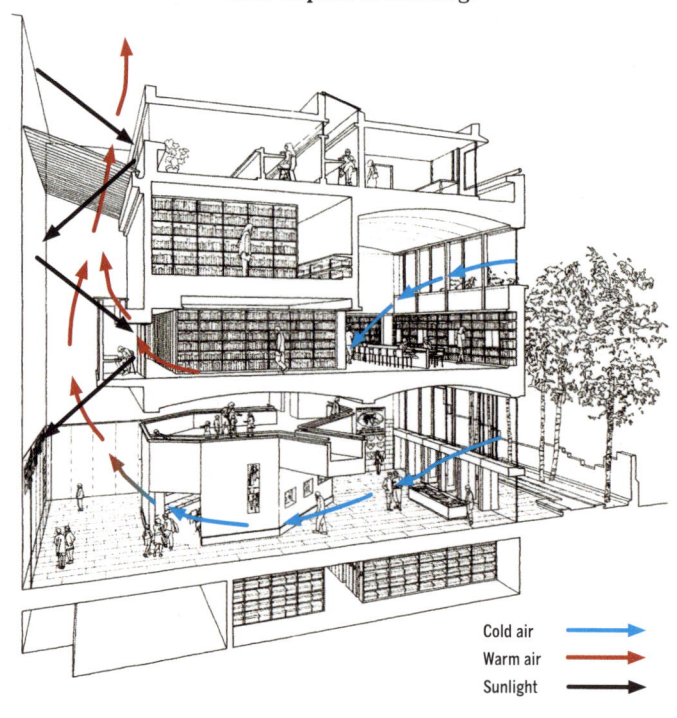

Cold air →
Warm air →
Sunlight →

see Vernacular 253

S Stairs

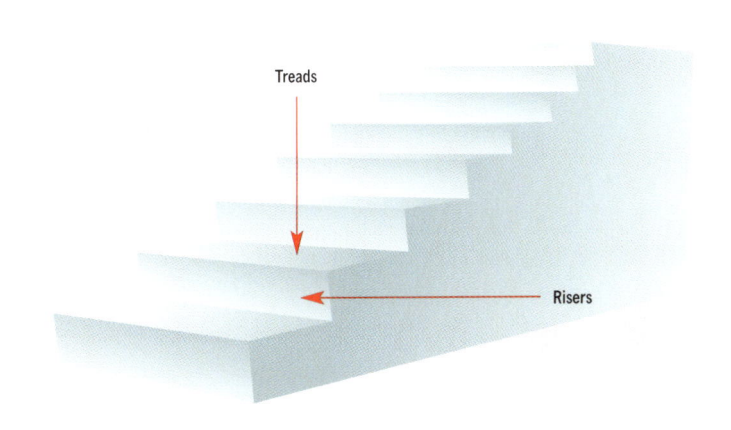

Treads

Risers

The most common means of movement between floor levels in a building. A stair consists of the horizontal 'goings' or treads and the vertical 'risers'. Stairs or staircases within a domestic environment are primarily simple cranked wooden constructions. However, the design can be more extreme and become the focal point of a space; for instance, they can be simple cantilevered treads enigmatically climbing up a wall, or conversely, a solid, hard-wearing element of poured reinforced concrete.

see Cantilever 46, Domestic 77

S Starck, Philippe

The famous and prolific French designer who has designed almost everything from interiors and buildings to mass-produced objects such as chairs, kitchenware and motorbikes. He is in a group of artist/designers called New Design, although Starck concerns himself more with the production of everyday objects rather than exclusive one-off art pieces. As such he has worked for clients as diverse as the United States Navy, Alessi, the former French President François Mitterrand and the US discount store chain Target. Pictured is Starck's foyer of the Royalton Hotel in New York, USA.

see Alessi 19

S Structure

A typical masonry load-bearing structure, such as Edinburgh Castle (pictured right) creates different interior spaces to that of a steel-frame span structure, such as the Gothic train shed of St Pancras International, London (pictured above).

Structure can be described as a collection or assemblage of materials that when joined together will withstand the loads and forces to which they are subjected. These loads are not confined to just the weight of the building itself, but will also include forces such as wind, people, furniture and fittings. There are two basic methods of construction: load bearing and frame. The load-bearing structure is thick and heavy and generally constructed from bricks or stone blocks built up from the ground. This type of structure creates small confined spaces due to the restricted span of the roof or floor beams, and the windows are of a limited size. The frame structure is constructed from a series of columns and beams, usually organised in a grid formation, which take the weight of the building; they can be made from concrete, steel or timber. This type of structure creates large open spaces.

see Beam 38, Load Bearing 150, Window 263

S Surface   238

Surface can be used to connect the building with its context. The rammed earth wall of the remodelled Chapel of Reconciliation in Berlin, Germany contains fragments of the old building, reinforcing its connection with the past.

The tactile element that establishes a direct relationship between human contact and the building. The surface of any element, that is, the specific materials from which it is made, determines the very character of the building. We can experience a space through the surface of the objects or elements within it; these elements may be hot or cold, hard or soft, new or old, rough or smooth. When a building is reused it is a common technique to juxtapose the existing surfaces with the new elements, to create a contrast between old and new.

see Insertion 128, Space 233

S Sustainability 239

The BedZED housing estate in England consists of a series of living/working units that combine sustainable technologies, such as grey water recycling and solar power, with energy-conserving building techniques.

The sensible use of natural resources in the construction and design industry so that materials are not depleted or used in an unnecessary or wasteful way. It also refers to methods of construction using certain materials that do not contribute to climate change through the exhaustion of natural resources or their transportation across the world. Within interior architecture, the term can also be defined as a structure that is spatially flexible and can sustain a number of redesigns.

see Ethics 97, Materials 160–161, Structure 237

S Symmetry 240

SYMMETRY IS THE PROCESS OF MIRRORING ONE SIDE OF AN OBJECT OR BUILDING WITH THE OPPOSITE SIDE. IT IS A COMMON FEATURE OF CLASSICAL ARCHITECTURE, IN WHICH BOTH THE FAÇADE AND THE INTERNAL ORGANISATION ARE OFTEN SYMMETRICAL. ITS ANTONYM IS ASYMMETRY, A DEVICE COMMONLY EMPLOYED IN DECONSTRUCTIVIST DESIGN WHERE THE VARIOUS PARTS OF THE BUILDING ARE INTENTIONALLY DIFFERENT.

☞ see Classical 52, Deconstruction 70, Façade 99

T Tactics   241

Tactics are the elements that come together to create the character of an interior or building. It is the combination of these elements that distinguish or make different one place from another. The elements give character: they define the quality and provide the features of a building, and it is this tactical deployment that gives the interior its individual nature.

Tactics such as this Gothic staircase in the Lello Bookshop in Porto, Portugal, can establish the character of an interior.

☛ see Detail 73, Element 88

T Tension 242

A type of structural technique that uses stretched elements to create structural integrity. For example, a feature staircase such as the one shown here can be constructed from a series of tensely stretched wires that support transparent glass treads. The stretched elements combined with the compressed elements create structural integrity.

The tensile steel and glass staircase in the London flagship Joseph shop, by Eva Jiřičná.

👉 see Jiřičná, Eva 137

T Textile Design

243

The design of fabrics or textiles has a powerful influence on an interior. The choice of textile design when decorating can produce a distinct effect upon the mood of the space. A heavily patterned or busy design will be complex and perhaps deliberately overwhelming whereas a simple design is calmer and more subtle. Textiles are used within interiors not just for the soft furnishings and fittings, but in a much more architectural manner, perhaps as a set of huge atrium-sized curtains, or even as an integral component within the design of the façade. Illustrated below are just some of the pattern treatments given in textile design.

Ethnic
A design with a theme that echoes foreign or exotic cultures and landscapes.

Conversational
A pattern that features repeated everyday objects or creatures.

Paisley
The paisley design is a well-known design and features flower and leaf motifs.

All over
A design that works all over the fabric and dominates the background colour.

Ditsy
Small motifs on a simple background.

Chinoiserie
Eurpoean designs that feature elements of Chinese culture and landscape such as lanterns, willow trees and pagodas.

T Texture 244

Soft, felt display elements contradict the hard Russian oak flooring of the interior of OKI-NI.

Texture describes the exact quality of how an object feels: rough, smooth, soft, hard, for example. It can be also used to describe the quality or character of a space. The texture of a space can be manipulated using artefacts as well as materials to suggest certain ideas or to make cultural references.

☛ see Materials 160–161, Space 233

T Theatre Design

245

A particular form of interior architecture and design. The theatre, while being a social and public space, has added technical considerations such as acoustics, lighting and sightlines, which result in a complex design process. The front-of-house area such as the box office, reception and bar are social and functional. Meanwhile, the back of house, including the backstage area, dressing rooms and fly tower, have complex requirements and are usually less ostentatious than the public areas. Pictured is the Vienna Opera House.

see Acoustics 18

T Threshold   246

The threshold between the interior and the exterior of Girona University in Spain is clearly marked by the gate.

Commonly used to refer to the entrance of a space, the threshold is the point at which one space becomes another. It is an important transition point within a building, and consequently, it receives a great deal of attention during the design process. It can mark the point between one condition and another, such as inside and outside, a small space to a large one, or darkness to light. The threshold is also the name for the door sill or doorstep, specifically marking the point at which one enters a building.

☞ see Door 79

T Truss 247

The strength of the truss is derived from its triangular form.

A framework usually constructed from a number of straight timber or steel elements that are joined together to bridge a gap. A common form is the triangular timber truss used in roof construction; the sloping sides of the trusses are supported on the top of the walls and take the weight of the roof, while the horizontal cross members stop the truss from splitting apart. Trusses can also be criss-crossed horizontal structures, tied together, top and bottom, by beams. Together they form a strong and stable structure.

see Beam 38, Structure 237

T Tudor

Commonly represented by the black-and-white half-timbered buildings constructed during the reign of the House of Tudor in England (1485–1603), Tudor design has been revived in modern house building as an attempt to inject a historical aesthetic into new suburban estates. Mock Tudor can be used as a decorative effect both within and on the exterior of the building.

Chester in England still retains many original Tudor buildings. Note the trademark black-and-white half timbering.

U Universal Design Studio

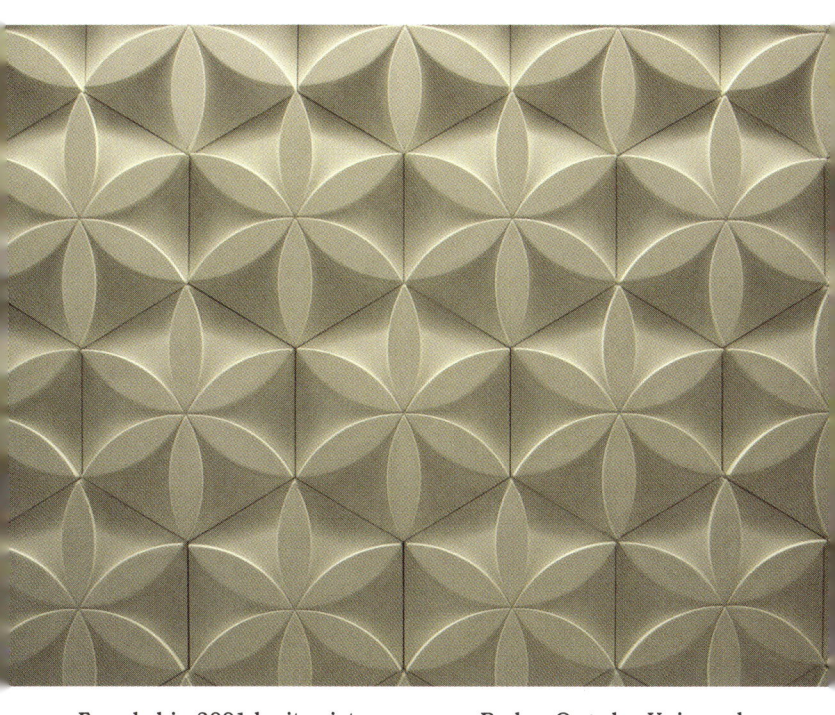

Founded in 2001 by its sister company Barber Osgerby, Universal Design Studio is a multidisciplinary office for industrial designers, interior designers and architects. Their recent work includes Damien Hirst's Pharmacy restaurant. They are also working on the redevelopment of Battersea Power Station and redesigning the Boiler House and Turbine Hall in the Tate Modern, UK. Their work can be described as embracing the contemporary aesthetic of clean lines, minimal junctions and applied monochromatic decoration. Pictured is the regular off-white relief that faces the Stella McCartney shop, typical of the stripped modernist approach taken by Universal Design Studio.

U Urbanism

The science, study and design of urban areas. Urbanism is a term commonly used to describe not only the process of town planning, but also the development of much smaller urban areas. It implies a greater depth of understanding of the social and cultural factors that affect urban environments. Urban design is an all-encompassing idea and more than planning; it is related to context, people and social requirements. Illustrated is Meeting House Square in Dublin, Ireland. This public space is at the centre of the regeneration of the previously run-down Temple Bar district.

see Postmodernism 193

U Utopia

From the Greek où that translates as 'not' and tópos that means 'place', the literal meaning is 'nowhere', as Utopia is the imagined ideal world or society. Many modernists believed that Utopia could be created through the application of specific design principles. The utopian ideals of the planners and architects who built housing in Britain during the post-war era are now considered to be outdated and, in some areas, disastrous. The rapid demise of the new society they tried to create led to the creation of Utopia's opposite, dystopia, which described the crime-ridden estates their visions had become. Pictured is the Barbican Housing estate in London, England, which, when built in the 1960s, was regarded as the future vision for inner-city housing developments.

see Modernism 168–169

V Ventilation 252

Ventilation describes the process of air movement through a building and can be achieved through either artificial or natural systems. Natural ventilation is the most common form; air movement is produced through windows that open.

Within sealed buildings (those without opening windows) or those that have massive floor plates, ventilation is provided by artificial air-conditioning systems that circulate the air though ducts.

Illustrated are the vents of the air conditioning system in the Basement Project of the Science Museum, London. The vents themselves are deployed as striking features of the interior as well as being elements of mechanical engineering.

☞ see Cooling 62, Environmental Control 95, Heating 122

V Vernacular 253

This church in East Anglia in the UK is typical of a structure built in an environment that is short of large pieces of stone, hence the use of local flint as infill.

A type of architecture and design of a particular given time and place. This style uses locally available materials to reflect the environmental, cultural, traditional and historical contexts of the location in which a building is erected. Thus the vernacular architecture of North Africa is made from local resources, mud and stone with a minimal use of timber and designed with small windows and thick walls to resist the local hot and dry climate. The vernacular architecture of the Lake District in England is houses built from local stone, with sloping roofs to repel the rain and small windows to keep out the wind.

see Context 61

V Victorian

The grand entrance hall of the Natural History Museum in London is a testament to both Victorian engineering and the eclectic use of different styles of architecture.

The era in British history around the time of the reign of Queen Victoria (1837–1901). Although she did not come to the throne until 1837, the Victorian age is generally agreed to have culturally begun in 1832. It was a period of great advance in British technology, industry and expansion. A fantastic example of this period was the first World Fair held in the glass and steel cathedral of Crystal Palace in Hyde Park, London, in 1851. Known as the Great Exhibition, it showcased British ingenuity and manufacturing industries. It was a period in architecture that was symbolised by great opulence and the construction of Britain's great museums along with some of its best-known public buildings.

V View   255

A view is usually an image of a scene, typically a pleasant picture through an opening within an interior or through the exterior wall of a building. The view into and out of an interior is a useful tactic in interior design and can enhance the experience of a particular space.

The view across a bridge and through the interior of the Old Masters pavilion of the Groninger Museum, the Netherlands, facilitates circulation and adds to the dynamism of the space.

☞ see Circulation 50, Tactics 241

V Villa

The term villa originated in ancient Rome to describe an upper-class country house. Today it is commonly used to describe a detached home found in mainland Europe or North America. Archetypal examples are the Villa Müller in Vienna by Adolf Loos, Villa Savoye near Paris by Le Corbusier and Farnsworth House in Illinois, USA, by Ludwig Mies van der Rohe (pictured).

see Le Corbusier 145, Loos, Adolf 151

V Vitra 257

Vitra are more renowned for their ambitious headquarters (shown here) than for the furniture they produce. Both their factory and headquarters are situated in Weil am Rhein, Germany, and the manufacturers have employed the world's most progressive architects to design the buildings. These included Frank Gehry, Zaha Hadid, Alvaro Siza and Tadao Ando, among others.

Vitra do not just concentrate on architecture, they have also acquired the rights to make a number of pieces of classic twentieth-century furniture, including designs by Philippe Starck, Jean Prouvé, Ron Arad and Charles and Ray Eames.

see Eames, Charles and Ray 85, Starck, Philippe 236

V Volume

258

The three-dimensional space enclosed within or occupied by an object. Individual spaces within a building can be referred to as volumes or the volume of the whole building can be referenced. For example, the Turbine Hall of the Tate Modern in London is an enormous volume of space that is used to display large-scale works of art. The model pictured represents the building's interior space. Each divided compartment is a room with individual spaces, which can also be referred to as volumes.

see Space 233

W Wall

Illustrated is a screen wall in a Japanese interior, which is used to separate the inside from outside while allowing light into the space.

The vertical plane that encloses space. A wall can be structural and made from brick, stone or concrete; or non-structural and made from perhaps glass, timber or even paper. A wall may be temporary or permanent; it may make a dramatic statement within the space or it may recede. The wall creates a boundary to the experience of the space.

☛ see Floor 101, Partition 182, Structure 237

W Wall Covering

Wall coverings are usually wallpapers or paint, but they can be made from many different materials: rubber, leather, plastics, metal, even fabric. They can help define the space and project an image of the function of a building. They are also used to conceal marks or imperfections on the surface of the wall. During various historical periods there have been fashions for different types of wall coverings. Enormous tapestries were traditionally hung in great northern European houses to provide both insulation and decoration. In the 1970s there was a brief trend for tongue-and-groove timber cladding on interior walls, reminiscent of a Scandinavian sauna. Now unusual materials such as fibre-optics or resins are used to decorate walls and create intriguing surfaces.

W Wharton, Edith

The American heiress and writer, who was also a respected interior and landscape designer (1862–1937) and trendsetter of her time. She wrote widely on these subjects, and is well known for her book, *The Decoration of Houses*, a sort of interior design manual in which she denounced Victorian interior design with its bric-a-brac and cluttered, opulent furniture. Wharton advocated clean interiors that were inspired by simple classicalism, accentuated by carefully selected furniture. Pictured is Wharton's self-designed home, The Mount (1902), in Massachusetts, USA.

see Classical 52, Victorian 254

W Whiteread, Rachel

A British installation artist who won the Turner Prize in 1993 for her controversial work, *House*. For this project she cast in concrete the inside of a Victorian terraced house, which had been earmarked for demolition. After the cast was made the house was pulled down, leaving only the positive impression of the negative space. Whiteread's tactic of casting negative spaces was repeated for her Vienna *Holocaust Memorial* (shown here), which leaves the viewer to consider not the structure, but the emptiness of the space that we occupy.

W Window

A window provides natural light and views in and out of a space. The frame, which can be made of varying materials, usually holds panes of glass that provide a solid transparent opening within a solid structure. The window has two main purposes: to admit light and to provide a view – although the latter is not always provided. Windows are used variously in shops and restaurants to give views into the building, enticing potential customers. Pictured is the highly decorated window of the Casa Batlló in Barcelona, Spain, by Antonio Gaudí.

see Framing 108, View 255

W Wolfe, Elsie de

This American interior decorator was a self-described 'rebel in an ugly world'. Wolfe (1865–1950) was reacting to the Victorian aesthetic with which she was brought up. It was through her interest in the design of stage sets that Wolfe entered the world of interior decoration. Her first, and perhaps still her most notable project, was the interior for the Colony Club, New York (1905) (pictured). This commission and collaboration with the building's architect and Wolfe's friend, Stanford White, resulted in the first social club for and by women.

see Victorian 254

W Wrapping

The wrapping of an element or building is the encasing of the object in a material that acts as a skin. In the case of reuse, wrapping may take the form of a new cladding over the existing skin of the building, which may be wrapped in a contrasting material to that of the original. This will highlight the changes and signal its rebirth and new function, as demonstrated in the picture above of the nearly completed wrapping of the Reichstag. Christo and Jean Claude encased the building in a new skin that symbolised its rebirth as the new parliament building for a unified Germany.

☛ see Cladding 51, Reuse 214

Wright, Frank Lloyd

An American master architect and designer and important member of the Chicago School, Frank Lloyd Wright (1867–1959) is best known for the Solomon R. Guggenheim Museum in New York, USA. His work was largely based on domestic architecture. His own home and studio at Taliesin, Wisconsin, where he schooled his apprentices, is a key example of his Prairie Architecture. Wright's designs attempted to incorporate the house itself into the landscape. Pictured is the interior of the Unity Temple in Illinois, USA.

X Xenakis, Iannis

A Greek interior designer who was also known as a composer. Xenakis (1922–2001) worked most notably with Le Corbusier on La Tourette, the monastery constructed in Eveux-sur-l'Arbresle, France, in 1960 (pictured). Xenakis was principally responsible for the interior of the Dominican monastery, creating the austere yet colourful and light space. He is also noted for his work on the Phillips Pavilion for the 1958 Brussels World Fair, a building that is usually attributed to Le Corbusier despite Xenakis's greater contribution to the design. The pavilion was described as less a building, more a multimedia experience.

see Le Corbusier 145

Y Yasui, Hideo

The Japanese interior designer and architect responsible for the design of some stunning retail spaces and private homes in Japan. He is known for his use and manipulation of artificial light with which he sculpts spaces, creating amazing effects. The display units in the D'Grace store in Tokyo, Japan (pictured), for example, are constructed from translucent plastic and have lights mounted behind the shelves, giving the products an ethereal glow.

see Light: Artificial 146, Retail Design 213

Y Yoshioka, Tokujin

A Japanese interior and product designer who uses lighting and unusual materials to create remarkable and extraordinary effects in his projects. Yoshioka initially worked with fashion designer Issey Miyake and one of his earlier projects was a store for the designer in Tokyo, Japan (pictured). Within this scheme he employed light as the creator of the space, controlling the colour, transparency and opaque nature of the wholly glazed shop front, enabling it to be easily reinvented. Nicknamed 'material boy', he encourages his clients and suppliers to be open-minded and inventive with materials.

see Light: Artificial 146, Materials 160-161

Z Zeitgeist

A German word that translates as 'the spirit of the age'. Zeitgeist is used in design and architecture to describe something that is in tune with the spiritual and aesthetic ideals of its age. For example, modernist architecture and interiors, which expressed the machine aesthetic and a purity of form typical of the modern industrial age, captured the zeitgeist of the period.

The Unité d'Habitation, Marseille, France, by Le Corbusier. This iconic modernist housing project exemplifies the zeitgeist of utopian post-war modernist architecture.

Z Zoomorphic

The act of applying any animalistic-inspired qualities to non-animal related objects such as furniture or buildings. Zoomorphic designs have the appearance of, or are obviously influenced by the qualities of animals, whether in the skeleton of a structure, in its movement or even in the actual form. Pictured is the 'Long Crawley Thing' designed by Carl Clerkin, a chair with a centipede-like form. Animalistic designs and motifs are commonly found in traditional Scandinavian design such as the ancient Viking longships. Zoomorphic designs were often employed in ancient cultures to represent ideas of power, wisdom and virility.

The Details

The Timeline

2BC
Roman
Roman architecture was largely derived from Greek architectural forms and adhered to formulaic designs and proportional systems. The creation of the wall allowed the Romans to develop the concept of the room as a recognised and useful space. The Pantheon is a fine example of a large room covered with a dome.

330–1400s
Byzantine
The architecture of the Christian Byzantine Empire is characterised by generous inner spaces, which are symmetrical and covered with large domes. Many remarkable examples of Byzantine architecture still exist today, mostly religious buildings. Of particular note is the Blue Mosque of Istanbul, formally the cathedral Hagia Sophia.

1420–1650s
Renaissance
Beginning in fifteenth-century Italy, Renaissance thinkers learnt from the texts of ancient Greek and Roman scholars, knowledge that had been lost for centuries in the Dark Ages. Greco-Roman architecture was revived as classical architecture. The Renaissance is said to have begun in Florence with the work of Brunelleschi.

1485–1603
Tudor
Most commonly represented by the black-and-white half-timbered buildings that evolved during the reign of the House of Tudor in England. Tudor buildings, in terms of interiors, are most noted for the concept of communal living in the form of a grand hall where nearly all activities took place.

1830s–1901
Victorian
An era of British history where architecture was symbolised by great opulence, optimism and ingenuity. It was a time that saw the construction of some of Britain's best-known public buildings. Industrialisation brought about the manufacture of cheaper goods and this is reflected within interiors that were heavily decorated and extremely ornate.

1850s–1890s
Arts and Crafts
A largely British and American movement that sought to develop a new form of moral design. The intention was to reinstate the skills of craftsmen within architecture and revive medieval methods of construction and habitation. This idea was taken to an extreme in the case of the Red House, in 1859.

1865–1950
Wolfe, Elsie de
American interior decorator who describes herself as a 'rebel in an ugly world'. She was reacting to the Victorian aesthetic with which she was brought up. She strove to create simple, elegant interiors that possessed an eighteenth-century French classical influence. Her most notable project was the interior for the Colony Club, New York, 1905.

1867–1959
Wright, Frank Lloyd
An American master architect, designer and important member of the Chicago School, Wright believed that a building should be a product of its place and time rather than an imposed style. This extended to the harmonious relationship between form, design and the function of the building.

1868–1928
Mackintosh, Charles Rennie
Mackintosh is noted for the Glasgow School of Art, a building that was constructed in two parts which show the development of his style. Mackintosh established a style that was uniquely his, drawing on beaux-arts training and modern influences, such as Arts and Crafts in England and art nouveau in France.

1870–1933
Loos, Adolf
Developer of the Raumplan spatial organisation system and an influential pre-modernist. Loos objected to unnecessary ornamentation and the excesses of the Victorian age. The Raumplan is a type of complex three-dimensional planning that provides a series of spaces with an internal focus and develops links between the interior rooms.

1878–1976
Gray, Eileen
Eileen Gray made her reputation as a designer of furniture, rugs and lacquered screens. She later gained fame as an architect and interior designer who created elegant and spare residences in the modernist style. She was recognised for her exhibit at the Paris Salon d'Automne in 1923.

1883–1952
Atkinson, Robert
A prolific British designer of the inter-war period, Robert Atkinson is most well known for his design of art deco cinemas. He designed the interior of the Daily Express building in London, which is typical of his style, with curving forms that dominated the 1930s Hollywood-inspired interior.

1887–1965
Le Corbusier
A leading proponent of the modernist architectural style and probably the most influential twentieth-century architect. Le Corbusier was a prolific writer and architectural theorist. *Vers une Architecture* [1923] and *Le Modulor* [1948] both theorised modern architecture and scale, while *Le Modulor* gave a frame of reference to the human form.

1890–1914
Art Nouveau
The reaction to the mass industrialisation and consumerisation of 'craft' that had taken place in the nineteenth century. Art nouveau embraced the ambiguity of the Impressionists and endeavoured to instil design with more fluid and natural forms. Hector Guimard is the creator of the famous graceful and flowing Paris Métro signs.

1890–1960
Modernism
An art, architecture and design movement that was shaped by the industrialisation and urbanisation of Western society. Modernism embraced an asymmetrical approach to layout – the abandonment of decoration in favour of geometric forms to create functional spaces. Modernists felt that architecture could create a utopian society.

1901–1914
Edwardian
A period of sober reflection upon the decorative excesses of Victorian design. The Edwardian era was the period when a long-time King-in-waiting was able to realise his many plans for the betterment of society. Much of the best regarded domestic architecture and urban planning in Britain is of this period.

1906–1973
Scarpa, Carlo
Scarpa was renowned for the sensitive manner in which he handled the relationship of the old to the new and the monumental to the everyday. He was the forerunner of an approach based upon a sympathetic understanding of the existing building and he is considered the greatest exponent of the art of remodelling.

1917–1930s
De Stijl
A Dutch design movement that brought together artists, designers and architects. De Stijl sought a pure abstraction through the reduction of all design to the essentials of form and colour with simple vertical and horizontal compositions. They advocated the use of clean planes decorated with primary colours.

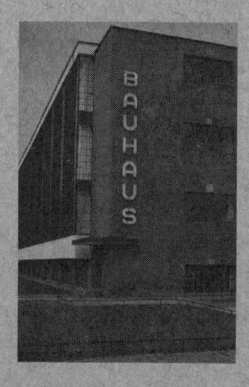

1919–1933
Bauhaus
A hugely influential school of architecture and design and a designers' collective based in Germany. It aimed to provide a fresh approach that focused on producing designs according to 'first principles'. The architecture and design produced by members of the Bauhaus rejected decorative detailing in favour of pure form without ornamentation.

1920–1930s
Art Deco
A branch of modernism, art deco was an aesthetic that attempted to depict the fast and streamlined nature of contemporary life. The name is derived from the Paris-based 1925 Exposition Internationale des Arts Décoratifs et Industriels Modernes.

1920s–1960s
Mies van der Rohe, Ludwig
A pioneer of modern architecture through his use of modern construction materials such as steel and glass, he advanced the international style, which is characterised by simplicity and clarity. He encapsulated the style with aphorisms such as 'God is in the details' and 'less is more'.

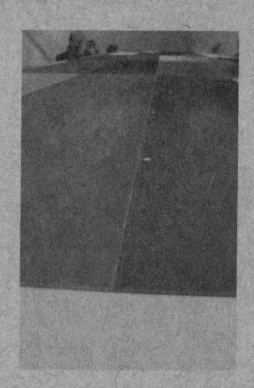

1928–1994
Judd, Donald
The American minimalist installation artist, Donald Judd, used clean platonic forms to create environments. He questioned the nature of the object, the space that it occupies and how we relate to them. He is seen as an extremely influential figure and sited as a forerunner of minimalist architecture and design.

1941–1950s
Utility
Due to wartime shortages, the British government introduced a range of basic domestic furniture called Standard Emergency Furniture that was aimed at people whose furniture had been destroyed in an air raid. This was largely made from tubular steel and plywood and the intention was to produce furniture of the highest quality from limited resources.

1949
Starck, Philippe
The French star designer who has produced many beautiful and eclectic designs, from architecture and interiors to mass-produced objects. He has the ability to transform the mundane everyday object into a collectible. He is responsible for the redesign of international hotels and places that have become almost as important as tourist destinations.

1950s–present
Minimalism
A form of art, design and architecture that emerged in the 1950s based upon pure and clean forms. The use of sheer surfaces, limited colour palette and absolutely minimal detail has come to be perceived as the height of good taste. This has become a much followed movement.

1960s–present
Postmodernism
A creative movement that questions the very notion of a reliable reality through deconstructing and engaging in the ideas of fragmentation and incoherence, along with the plain ridiculous. The antithesis of, and reaction to modernism, postmodernism has been described as the architecture of Western capitalism.

1970s
Brutalism
Brutalist architecture uses hard, angular, geometric forms and has a raw unfinished concrete aesthetic. It was a popular form of architecture used by municipal authorities in Britain for everything from bus stations to housing and became wildly unpopular with the British public by the end of the 1970s.

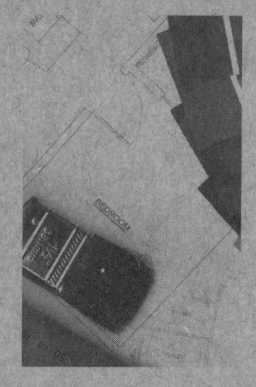

1970s–present
Contextualism
A movement that started as a reaction to modernism, and the destruction of urban environments. In an attempt to stem the demolition and devastation that occurred in most Western cities, contextualism attempts to create architecture and design that is integrated into its environment rather than fighting it.

1980s–present
Deconstruction
A branch of postmodern architecture, design and theory characterised by ideas of fragmentation and non-linear design processes. It is based on the concept that language is inherently unstable and can be read in a number of different ways depending upon the position of both the author and the reader.

1990s
TV Makeovers
Changing Rooms led the vanguard that popularised interior decoration in the late 1990s. It was aspirational television and made stars of the presenters who inspired a generation of MDF users. Various broadcasters across the world have copied the format of the programme.

Credits

P 7, Image courtesy of Nigel Young / Foster + Partners
P18, Image courtesy of Sarah Duncan
P19, 197, 232, Image courtesy of Alessi S.p.a., Crusinallo, Italy
P23, Image courtesy of Stephen Mills
P29, Image courtesy of Charlotte Wood/Arcaid.co.uk
P30, 277, Image courtesy of Max Alexander
P37, Image courtesy of Mark Fiennes/Arcaid.co.uk
P46, Image courtesy of Thijs Wolzak, Amsterdam
P55, Image courtesy of Arch. Ignazia Favata - Studio Joe Colombo Milano
P65, Image courtesy of Michaela O'Hare
P67, Image courtesy of Studio Ilse
P68, Image courtesy of Design: Constantin and Laurene Boym
Produced by Boym Partners Inc; Photo courtesy of Boym Partners Inc
P69, Image courtesy of Claire Gordon Interiors
P78, Photographer: Brigid Smith, image courtesy of Stephen Donald Architects
P80, Photographer: Farshid Assassi
P81, Images courtesy of: Graeme Brooker; Laura Empsall; Daisy Klyhn
P82, Bar Europe for droog / The European Council by Bas van Tol.
Photographer: Jonas de Witte © 2008 Droog; A Human Touch (droog)
Shenzhen, 2006. Photograph by Davide Quadrio © 2008 Droog
P88, Photographer Hans-Jürgen Landes and image courtesy of Behnisch
Architekten
P89, Image courtesy of Steve Batty
P98, © Land Design Studio / Photography Lee Mawdsley
P103, Image courtesy of Bullring Birmingham, Shopping Centre
P107, Image courtesy of Nigel Young / Foster + Partners
P116, Image courtesy of Mark Fiennes/Arcaid.co.uk
P118 Image courtesy of Richard Bryant/Arcaid.co.uk
P121, Image courtesy of Inga Knoelke/Imagekontainer
P123, Image courtesy of John Hejduk Fonds
Collection Centre Canadien d'Architecture/Canadian Centre
for Architecture, Montréal
P136, Image courtesy of Gertrude Jekyll Collection (1955-1)
Environmental Design Archives, University of California, Berkeley
P137, Image courtesy of Robert K Wilson
P140, Image courtesy of Kda, Photographer Jun Takagi
P141, Image courtesy of Yves Klein
P143, Image courtesy of Brutele, Lucien Kroll

P144, © Land Design Studio / Photography Nick Wood
P154, Image courtesy of Interior retail design by Callum Lumsden
P156, Image courtesy of Mark Fiennes/Arcaid.co.uk
P158, © Photo SCALA, Florence
P159, Image courtesy of Jacques Villion etching supplied by Hugh Little
P165, Image courtesy of Stepan Bartos
P167, Image courtesy of Alex Johnson
P169, © Peter Cook / View
P171, Image courtesy of Jeremy Cockayne/Arcaid.co.uk
P174, © The Royal Pavilion, Libraries and Museums, Brighton & Hove
P175, Image courtesy of Fabio Novembre. Photographer: Settimio Benedusi
P177, Photograph by Benny Chan, Fotoworks
P190, Image courtesy of Cassina Collection; Designer: Gio Ponti; Photographer: Ruy Texeira
P194, Image courtesy of Paul Warchol
P196, Image courtesy of Alan Weintraub/Arcaid.co.uk
P204, Image courtesy of George Cserna
P205, Photographer: Farshid Assassi
P206, Quote cited from: http://www.galinsky.com/buildings/villamueller/index.htm
P207, Image courtesy of Richard Bryant/Arcaid.co.uk
P209, Image courtesy of Reichen et Robert & Associés
P210, Image courtesy of Merkx + Girod
P212, Image courtesy of Dominic Roberts
P213, Photographer: Andy Barlow, Image courtesy of Rawfish Design Consultants
P215, Image courtesy of Florian Monheim/Bildarchiv-Monheeim/Arcaid.co.uk
P224, Image courtesy of Alex Johnson
P225, Image courtesy of Rachel Vallance
P231, Design by Softroom and Virgin Atlantic in house design team Photographer Richard Davies
P239, Image courtesy of BedZed
P242, Image courtesy of Richard Bryant/Arcaid.co.uk
P243, Images courtesy of Jenny Udale (Conversational, Paisley and All over), Furphy Simpson (Ditsy and Chinoiserie) and Joan Kerrigan (Ethnic)
P244, Image courtesy of David Grandorge
P256, Image courtesy of Alan Weintraub/Arcaid.co.uk
P269, Image courtesy of Nacasa & Partners Inc
All other images courtesy of Graeme Brooker and the authors

Conclusion

This book aims to enhance the understanding and appreciation of interior architecture and design by defining and explaining the many terms used within the disciplines, in addition to providing an insight into some of the historic and cultural contexts that have shaped their development.

We hope that this book helps you to better understand a new and ever-evolving set of principles that govern these disciplines and appreciate the concepts behind the different styles and influences upon interior architecture and design.

The work of Ben Kelly, such as the Basement Museum at the Science Museum, London, (pictured above) continues to serve as an exemplar of interior architecture and design.

Acknowledgements

Special thanks to all those who helped with the finding of the images, defining the terms, and those who provided the inspiration for some of the entries in this book.

In addition, Michael would like to thank Kate in particular for her unstinting support and encouragement throughout.

Graeme would like to thank Claire for her comfort and certainty.

And Sally would like to thank Reuben, Ivan and Agnes for their self-possession and Dominic Roberts for his encouragement.

A final thank you to everyone at AVA Publishing: Brian Morris, Renée Last, Caroline Walmsley, Leafy Robinson and in particular Sanaz Nazemi, for all of their help and assistance during the writing of this book.

Whilst this volume is by no means exhaustive, we have tried our best to include all those terms that are most commonly used in the realm of interior architecture. If you feel that we have missed any entries then please do let us know by sending us an email marked Visual Dictionary (Interior Architecture and Design) Entries to: enquiries@avabooks.co.uk. Please include your name and address, and if your entry makes it to an updated later edition of the book, we will send you a copy for free!

Index of Synonyms and Cross References

Adolf Meyer, 36
Aesthetic, 21, 28, 41, 43, 48, 134, 155, 179, 270
Alessi, 19, 68
Alteration, 135
Alvar Aalto, 126
Alvaro Siza, 257
Anaesthetics, 193
Andy Warhol, 119
Antonio Gaudí, 263
Arbeitsrat für Kunst, 36
Arrangement, 24
Augustus Pugin, 118
Barbican Estate, the, 251
Barcelona (German) Pavilion, 49, 189
Balustrade, 33, 34
Beaux-Arts, 156, 276
Bernini, 35
Berthold Lubetkin, 168
Body, 20
Cantilever, 46
Carpet, 102
Cartwright Pickard, 170
Caruso St John, 119
Castelvecchio, 101, 128, 173, 223
Ceramics, 51, 102, 190
Charles Gwathmey, 123
Charles Moore, 193
Charter Society of Designers (CSD), 201
Christo and Jean Claude, 265
Colonnade, 191
Commercial interior, 34
Communicate, 9, 195
Construction, 205
Contrasting, 21
Coop Himmelb(l)au, 32
Courtyard, 200, 233
Cubism, 27, 60
Daniel Libeskind, 70, 205
De La Warr Pavilion, 27
De Stijl, 72, 168, 172
Denys Lasdun, 41
Derelict, 162
Design Council, 139
Design Museum, the, 184
Device, 24
Diagram, 81, 188, 225
Dystopia, 251
Ecstacity, 54
Edouard Manet, 28
Edwardian, 37, 87
Environment, 25, 34, 40, 53, 61, 69, 84, 91, 95, 96, 126, 138, 168
Environmental, 10, 53, 62, 95, 130
Existing, 45
Feature, 18

Filippo Brunelleschi, 211, 274
Five Points of Architecture, 187
Frank Gehry, 104, 205, 257
Functionalism, 23,
Furniture, 113, 170
Future Systems, 103
Futurism, 27, 60
Gallery, 98
Garden, 31, 136, 233
Gerrit Rietveld, 72, 189
Gothic, 118, 202
Guggenheim Museum, 104, 266
Habitation, 42
Handrail, 34, 75
Hector Guimard, 28, 278
Herzog & de Meuron, 6, 166
Hill House, 37
House, 19, 198
Housing, 78, 168, 194
Human scale, 20
Identity, 40
Industry/Industrial, 22, 29, 43, 171, 220, 270
Installation, 74, 129, 135
Issey Miyake, 269
Jean Baudrillard, 127
Jean Prouvé, 257
John Pawson, 165
Joseph Rykwert, 199
Journal, 157, 190
Junction, 66, 229
Kevin Lynch, 86
Lázló Moholy-Nagy, 36
Le Modulor, 145
Lintel, 38, 192
Load, 22, 38
Louis Henri Sullivan, 106
Magazines 157, 190
Mechanisation, 155, 168
Mechanism, 50
Memphis collective, 232
Methodology, 78
Michael Graves, 19, 123
Museo Revoltella, 130
MVRDV, 46
Natural Form, 215
New Design, 236
Norman Foster, 23, 76, 114
Object, 176, 197
Olivetti, 232
Pantheon, 216
Participatory architecture, 143
Pediment, 191
Peter Eisenmann, 123
Philip Johnson, 134
Philip Webb, 29
Piet Mondrian, 72
Pompidou Centre, 95
Prairie Architecture, 266

Ramp, 75
Red House, 29
Regeneration, 100
Reinvention, 135
Residential, 43
Reveal, 135
Royal Institute of British Architects (RIBA), 231
Richard Meier, 123
Ron Arad, 257
Roof, 42, 237, 247
Routes, 124
Roy Lichtenstein, 119
Schröder House, 189
Seagram Building, 74
Shigeru Ban, 114
Shuttering, 41
Sightlines, 24
Sir John Soane, 207
Spatial, 186
Staircase, 33, 230, 242
Stairwell, 33, 178
Stanford White, 264
Star architect, 23
Stephen Holl, 126, 199
Style, 156
Tadao Ando, 257
Tate Modern, 154, 172, 233, 249, 258
Temporary, 69, 98
Theo van Doesberg, 72
Three-dimensional, 70, 81, 167, 185, 206
Two-dimensional, 185
Unité d'Habitation, 163, 270
Urban, 61, 250
Vers une Architecture, 145
Villa Rotunda, 181, 186, 227
Villa Savoye, 65, 169, 187, 256
Visuals, 81
Vladimir Tatlin, 60
Walter Gropius, 168
Wassily Kandinsky, 36
Will Alsop, 23
Yurt, 77, 84
Zaha Hadid, 23, 257